# Held at Gunpoint

## My Family's Trials and Triumphs in the Heart of Africa

by Sharon Rose Gibson

SG PUBLICATIONS
Siloam Springs, AR 72761
www.15minutewriter, www.sharonrosegibson.com


Book Layout ©2017 BookDesignTemplates.com


Held at Gunpoint: My Family's Trials and Triumphs in the Heart of Africa
Sharon Rose Gibson – 1st ed.
ISBN 978-1-954651-03-6

*This book honors my parents for their faithful response to God's call. My prayer is that this story will both encourage those following God's call and inspire others to answer His call to good works. I dedicate it to my children and grandchildren, future generations, and all who appreciate missionary stories of adventure, hardship, and faith.*

# Contents

# Introduction

*Everyone has stories to share and
someone needs to hear yours!*
SHARON ROSE GIBSON

She sat in her lounge chair after her teenage grandson left. "Whenever he visits, he's constantly on his phone. He doesn't even talk with me." She lamented. My heart went out to her.

During our family celebrations, when cell phones first became popular, I implored my family. "Look, we can use cell phones anytime. We're here to celebrate this special occasion together." They cooperated and at one of my birthday celebrations, one of my grandsons even told the other grandson to put his phone away. This pleased me to see him embracing our time together.

We live in a time where electronic devices dominate our lives. Almost everyone in the family has an electronic device, even the little ones.

Families used to sit around and talk, and the younger ones would listen to the older family members as they told their stories. I remember road trips when I was younger. We entertained ourselves by listening to our parents' stories. If we'd had electronic devices, we might not know some of those stories.

Now, we must make a conscious effort to pass down our stories and those of our parents to our descendants. When my grandsons were younger, I prayed for opportunities to share some of these stories. While that is good and important to share verbally, it's more permanent to write the stories down for them to read later and for future generations as well. This is the reason I am writing my stories about growing up in Africa. Now it's called The Democratic Republic of Congo, and my school was at Rift Valley Academy in Kenya, East Africa.

Though I talk about being held at gunpoint during and after Congo's tumultuous independence from Belgium, much of the book is about our life in Africa. I want to tell my children, grandchildren, future generations, and others who are interested in my missionary family's journey of love and care for those in Africa.

This is not a novel but vivid storytelling from my experiences, personal reflections and my parents' letters. I want to ensure their legacy is not lost.

They had some life threatening, harrowing times and extreme difficulties, but they also had triumphs. They did not live their lives in vain. Their care and work produced much fruit that remains to this day, decades later.

I hope you will see how faith shaped their lives. Because of my parents' faith, others were inspired to be triumphant in the difficulties they faced. I hope this book will also inspire you to grow in your faith and confidence in God's faithfulness.

The Bible admonishes us over and over to tell of the Lord's wonderful deeds. I listed out the verses that show this at the end of this book.

If you're not of my faith, I believe you will still find these stories interesting and inspiring. Also, I want to offer a disclaimer. Everything shared in this book may not be "politically correct" according to the modern-day lens. Please remember that this account reflects that era, which was culturally different from ours.

I haven't written this like a normal book. I've shared some unrelated memories, but I felt they were important to share to give you an understanding of what life was like. There are some gaps because I didn't have letters from my mom during the evacuation.

Included also are tributes to my mom and my dad. I've included photos from old slides and photo albums that were relevant. I wish I had more, but I hope they will give you an idea of our family and what life was like. I refer to my parents as mom and dad. Their names were Ernest and Virginia McFall.

Even though I've had this edited and proofread by several people, you may still find something that isn't clear or something I missed. Please email me at info(a)15minutewriter and kindly let me know so I can fix it.

Now that I've clarified these things, let's dive right into one of the more harrowing times.

# Held at Gunpoint
# Evacuation from Rethy

I whispered. "Shhhh! You're making too much noise. What if they come and see us here?" I admonished the other kids with me. We crouched outside the low windows underneath the building. We listened to the adults talk about the coming evacuation. We knew something was not right.

We didn't know too many details except that our dorm parents gave us a flat plastic bag. They told us to pack a change of clothes and underwear. This was in case we had to leave quickly and walk thirty miles north to the border of Sudan.

Congo had recently obtained its independence from the Belgians on June 30, 1960. My sister, Sandi, and I attended Rethy, a mission boarding school for grades 1-6.

It was 400 miles south of where my parents lived on a mission station. There, they taught and cared for the African people.

When Lumumba came to power as the first prime minister, our lives were threatened. He sought the communists for help. He strongly expressed anti-western, anti-European and anti-Capitalist sentiments. All the experienced Belgian administrators and technicians fled the country. This crippled both the economy and the government. Without the police and army officers, it was impossible to maintain order. The United Nations (UN) sent in troops to evacuate all the missionaries.

I didn't want to leave. I loved Rethy, the mission school where we climbed the trees, played and studied. Rethy's setting in the green hills with lush grass provided a scenic view. But the day came when the UN troops arrived. We grabbed our few belongings and headed to our appointed cars. One hundred and forty-six missionaries and children lined up ready to go.

My parents could not come down from their mission station to come get us. So, my dorm parents assigned me to another family. The man complained loudly that my parents did not come to go with us. He shouted in front of me, "What kind of parents don't come to take responsibility for their daughter?"

Any reassurance that I would be cared for and protected left me that day. At age twelve, the situation traumatized me enough. His reaction to taking responsibility for my care confused me. This threw me into a pit of fear with trauma chains that would bind me for years.

We climbed in the cars and headed on into the narrow deep forest roads. We drove out of the heavy trees and into the open. I looked out the window and saw the road behind us wrapped around the hills. The large caravan of cars on the winding roads intrigued me. I couldn't see the end, or the beginning of the cars.

Eventually, we reached the border, and the cars lined up where soldiers held us for hours. They carried machine guns and paced up and down past all the cars. As I watched them, once more, I feared for our lives. Then the man who drove our car got out. He started yelling at the soldiers. His outburst of anger terrified me further. What was he doing? Didn't he know they carried guns and could kill us? Even at the tender age of twelve, I knew his hot-headed reaction was not a good idea. Fortunately, nothing came about because of the man's tirade.

Still, we waited in the heat of the day. We watched the soldiers march by the cars, their guns poised and ready to shoot us. As I watched them, my heart raced, and my body trembled. I feared for our lives.

The wait dragged on for hours. We got out of the cars under adult supervision and went to an open area. My sister, Sandi, played with a hula hoop and other kids took turns. The African soldiers stood around watching, fascinated with the hula hoop. The playful environment lightened the tension. Some of the soldiers began to relax. Later, a missionary said it was my sister playing with the hula hoop that caused the soldiers to relax.

Finally, late at night, the soldiers let us go. We drove over the border. The Red Cross stood at a table handing out sandwiches. They had set up cots for us in a refugee camp. That was the one moment I felt cared for. An immense burden rolled off my young shoulders like a backpack of fear tumbling to the ground. The crowded conditions and cots lined up didn't matter. Our lives were spared. We were safe!

Yet, we had no radio contact with my parents. I didn't know whether my parents were dead or alive.

# A Safe Refuge –
# Arrival at RVA

After we safely crossed the border, the caravan drove to the Rift Valley Academy (RVA), a mission school near Nairobi, Kenya, East Africa. They set up a refugee camp separate from the school. I felt like an outsider, terrified and alone. My sister and I and the rest of the evacuated students were isolated from the main school campus.

For several months, I didn't know if my parents were dead or alive. I woke in the night screaming from nightmares. Unfortunately, back then, no one knew how to deal with trauma. They didn't know how to listen empathetically to my distress and how to bring healing. They didn't know I needed to hear comforting words and the comfort of scriptures. In that lack of comfort, I buried that trauma and those feelings. The nightmares continued to haunt me for years. I finally found healing from the trauma in my later adult years.

Eventually, word came that my parents were okay. They drove to RVA and stayed in Nairobi until it was safe to go back to Congo. I later learned from my mother that when they prayed and sought the Lord, He had given them Psalm 91. God told them to stay where they were. He especially spoke to them through verse 7, "A thousand may fall at your side, ten thousand at your right hand, but it will not come near you."

This literally happened to them. People were killed around them, but they were spared. Psalm 91 has since become one of my favorite Psalms. I've memorized it and have prayed it over my family and myself regularly. In the midst of the trauma we endured, we found refuge in the shadow of His wings. Psalm 91 is a wonderful heritage of protection passed down to me by my parents.

After several months, the administration moved all of us who had evacuated up with the rest of the kids at RVA. Fortunately, they welcomed us. We integrated into the community. I made some close friends. RVA became a refuge from the turmoil. My life at RVA ended up being rich and one of the most satisfying seasons of my life because of the activities, friends and good staff.

From the front porch of our dorm, we had a scenic view of the expansive Rift Valley with the volcanic mountain of Longonot. We even went on a group hike one time to the top of Longonot. The hike was exhausting yet exhilarating. When we reached the top, we enjoyed the magnificent view.

One time when I was on my way to school in a small plane with my friend, we flew over Lake Nakuru. We could hardly see the lake because of all the beautiful pink flamingoes.

The 7200 feet of elevation of Kijabe (the name of the town where the Rift Valley Academy was located) created mild weather year around. We wore sweaters in the morning and by noon, we didn't need them.

Sharon and friend, Ruthie Schuitt in RVA uniforms.

Everyone wore grey jumper type uniforms with the RVA emblem on it. We could wear any color of sweater or belt.

Throughout the academic year, we went to school for three months and then flew home for a month. MAF flew my friend and me to the Uganda border, the country next to Congo.

MAF (Missionary Aviation Fellowship) is an airplane mission. They are devoted to flying supplies to missionaries. At other times, when MAF couldn't take us, we'd fly on East African Airlines.

My father picked me up at the small airstrip. Then he drove us to our assigned mission station. My sister, Sandi, had gone back to Rethy with the younger

Sharon and Ruthie getting on the
plane to go to school.

grades, but their schedule was the same, so we were together on breaks at our parents' home. Later, when she was older, she also went to RVA. My parents were first assigned to Dungu, then Niangara, and last, Adi in Northeastern Congo. We had a joyous reunion every time. Mom made homemade donuts and cinnamon rolls to celebrate. When we drove up to the house, I can still remember the delicious aroma of cinnamon, as well as the joy on my mother's face when she saw us.

I enjoyed being home with my parents and sisters. I read a lot, but as a teenager, after a while I became bored. Though I loved my parents, toward the end of the month, I eagerly looked forward to going back to school. I enjoyed my friends and the activities.

Every time we drove to the Uganda border to go back to school at RVA, we faced the mechanical challenges. The rut ridden red dirt roads were difficult

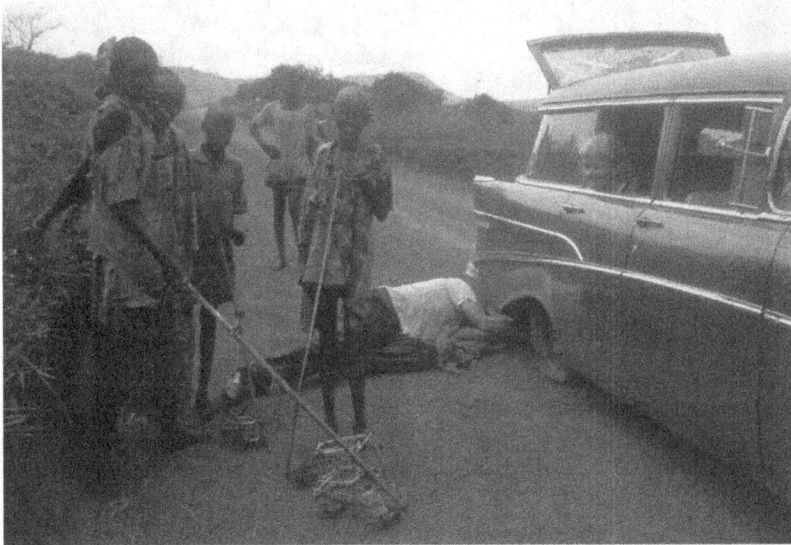

for our car to maneuver. Keeping a vehicle running on rough dirt roads is not easy. Dad constantly had to fix our vehicles. We had to drive slowly, so it took much longer to get anywhere. The red dirt blew everywhere. We had to wear scarves to keep our hair from being caked with dust. Later, we got a truck which was easier to manage.

Dad was not mechanically inclined. He had more scholarly gifts, but he had to learn to repair vehicles for survival.

Additionally, after the evacuation, armed soldiers stopped us at the border and sometimes on the roads.

They went through our things. They thought we were smuggling things out of the country. They pulled everything out to examine it. Sometimes it embarrassed my mom and us girls as they pulled out personal feminine items.

Broken down vehicles and border stops made travel difficult, and it took a long time to travel anywhere. The chaos continued in Congo through the next four years, and at various times, our lives were in danger. The soldiers held us at gunpoint many times, sometimes with a narrow escape. Some of those I'll share in another chapter.

But then I'm getting ahead of myself. How we ended up in Congo is an intriguing story.

# Extraordinary Call for Ordinary People

My younger sister and I sat in the back as the car lurched along at 20-30 miles per hour over deeply rutted mud roads in the jungles of Africa. We would ride these roads back and forth to the mission school. We went to school for three months. Then we went home to my parents' mission station for a month. To entertain ourselves, my sister and I picked out shapes in the clouds and called them out to each other.

Other times we'd ask mom and dad to tell us stories. Our favorite one was about when they got together. "Tell us about when you met," we would ask them with a sense of excitement over the intrigue of the story.

My mom and dad would grin. They gave each other the look that sweethearts give when they recall special

Ernest in the Navy.

Virginia

moments. My dad started. "We met at a church play at a Methodist church. I thought she was such a beautiful girl, and I couldn't believe she was interested in me!"

Then my mom chimed in, "I thought he was so handsome! We started dating, but his mother didn't like me. She put so much pressure on him, so we broke up before he went in the navy." (Later the mother came to accept her.)

Dad continued, "We still wrote to each other while I was in the navy. Then I met a man from the Navigator's organization. He helped me to see that going to church would not save me and send me to heaven. I realized I was a sinner and needed to accept Christ as my Savior and be born again by God's spirit. I accepted Christ and started studying the Bible with him as the man discipled me."

Mom piped in, "In the meantime, I also heard the same message about how I was a sinner. I needed to accept the Lord as my personal Savior, so I did. I decided to go to Bible school.

So, I wrote your dad a letter and told him I could no longer date him because I wanted to marry a Christian man."

Dad smiled. "I wrote her a similar letter and told her I could no longer date her because I wanted a Christian woman. Our letters crossed in the mail. We were both so happy when we got each other's letters." My dad smiled and continued.

Ernest and Virginia get engaged.

"My older sister wrote to me and sent me a photo of your mother in the letter. The newspaper published that she was going to go to Bible school. My sister said, 'Here's that girl you used to date. Good thing you don't date her anymore because she went and got religion.' Dad smiled, "I was so happy to hear this!" Both my parents chuckled. (Later the mother and family came to accept the marriage.)

My mom shared, "One day, your dad was due to come home from the war. In one of my Bible classes, I sat and wrote Mrs. Ernest McFall, Virginia McFall, all over my notebook. I looked up and saw your dad standing in the doorway. He was so handsome in his sailor uniform. I was so excited! He had come home from the war (WW2). He waited until I got out of class. We got engaged that night on March 26 and married July 4, 1946."

Ernest and Virginia engaged.

My sister and I entered the romance of the moment and savored every detail of the story. Every time we asked, they shared the story over and over and we loved it.

However, this ended up not only being a romance story. This was a union that would make a significant difference for many, since they lived a life of service.

My father and mother had simple upbringings. My father grew up in a small town in Girard, Kansas. He used to help the milkman deliver milk door to door when he was in school. His mother was married but her husband died, so then she married my father's dad. Unfortunately, he died when my father was eight, so my dad grew up fatherless. He had seven brothers and sisters.

My mother grew up in Wichita, Kansas. She had one sister, Juanita. I remember her telling us about how her dad went door to door selling. He wanted his daughters to have good clothes during the Great Depression. This showed her father's care for his family and his work ethic. Later, after the depression, he got into real estate, and he prospered. She told us she had a closet full of clothes and shoes, which she later gave up to go to the mission field.

Ernest and Virginia get married.

They met and got married in Wichita, Kansas. After they married, they sat in church one day listening to a missionary from Congo in Africa. He shared about the serious need for missionaries. This was a life altering moment for my parents.

My father felt moved by God's spirit that he was to go. He later told my mother, "I feel called to go to the Belgian Congo, Africa. But I want you to seek God and make sure you feel called as well. If you don't, you'll just be a missionary's wife."

So, my mom spent some time praying. She felt God calling her as well. They both responded to the verse, "And I heard the voice of the Lord saying, 'Whom shall I send, and who will go for us?' Then I said, "Here am I! Send me." (Isaiah 6:8 KJV)

My mom and dad were ordinary people. Because of God's call on their life, they did extraordinary things. They influenced many people in a positive way.

After this confirmation, they both went to Bible School at Midwest Bible College in St. Louis, Missouri. They left my baby sister, and me at two years old with my grandmother and aunt in Wichita.

After completing Bible College, they raised support. They visited churches to share the vision God had given them. They prepared to go overseas. I was four years old, and my sister, Sandi, was two years old. If you can imagine it, Mom had to plan clothes for the next five years for us. Typically, back then, missionaries went for five years. Then they came home for a year to meet with their supporters. My parents, my sister and I went over by ship, and they packed everything in barrels to protect the items they shipped.

First, though, my parents, my sister, Sandi and I went to Belgium for a year to learn French. Both my sister and I learned French easily because we were children.

French was the trade language for Congo. A trade language is the language everyone who trades learns to speak. The reason for this is that in Congo, every tribe speaks a different language. The Democratic Republic of Congo, then the Belgian Congo, is about 1/3 the size of the United States. But it had over 200 different tribes all speaking their own language. This would make it impossible to trade goods. Therefore, there is always a trade language to facilitate business.

# Growing Up in the Jungle

These are random, unconnected but interesting memories of growing up in the jungle.

I can still see the Africans running to our car. They smiled, cheered, and waved their hands! "Mama,

Dad discipled and taught the men. Some became pastors and established churches in the jungle.

Papa," they would cry out. This happened every time we went away on a trip and returned home to the mission station. They valued the teaching my dad gave them about God and the Bible.

Mom taught the women to read, and she used flannel graph lessons to share stories from the Bible.

Mom teaching the women.

She also taught them hygiene to prevent disease and how to care for their homes. They welcomed the care and wisdom my parents gave them in practical ways. They appreciated the way my parents cared for them spiritually, emotionally, and physically.

My mother taught me to appreciate their different cultural practices. One interesting cultural practice is that the Africans would never knock on our door. They stood outside a window and politely coughed until we went out to find out what they wanted.

They would often come to get medicine that my mother would give them, such as "itch medicine" that relieved itching from bug bites. My mother was not a nurse, but sometimes she helped the nurse at our station. We were fortunate to have a nurse because not every mission station had one. My mother even helped her deliver babies occasionally.

I remember one poignant time when an African mother died in childbirth. I can still see her laying there as she passed from life to death. It was common for the women to die in childbirth, though with the nurse there, she helped a lot of them live who would not have otherwise. It was common for babies to die because of all the diseases. We didn't have doctors anywhere close to us.

Another interesting cultural difference is the way the women carried the heavy loads while the men walked beside them empty-handed. The women were adept at carrying large loads and water on their heads.

The Africans built the houses on the mission station for the missionaries, the churches, and any other buildings we needed. They had a mindset, "If we don't get it done today, we'll get it done tomorrow." This mentality frustrated my dad because it took forever to build things.

The African women carried heavy loads on their heads.

The women worked in the fields with the men all day with their babies tied to their backs and then they would fix an evening meal. They only ate one meal a day at night. They harvested the rice and then pounded it to get the outer husk off so it would be edible. Often the teenagers and young girls did the pounding.

African girls pounding the rice.

Then they would put the rice in a flat basket-like container and shift it back and forth to blow away the chaff. Once the rice was separated from the husk it was to ready to cook.

On our way to get to our mission station in the jungle, we had to drive on extremely narrow roads. On one side, there was a steep mountain and on the other side, a sharp drop off the cliff. The roads were so narrow that on certain days of the week, you could drive one way one day and the next day you could drive the other way.

My sister, Sandi and I pounding the rice.

On the weekends, you could take your chances. Every time you went around a curve, you would lean on the horn to let anyone coming the other way know that you are coming. To say it was a harrowing experience is an understatement. As a child, I didn't worry about it because my dad was driving. I trusted him, so I felt safe. As an adult, I don't think I could do it!

At that time, we had a truck because it was the only vehicle that could take the rutted roads. My sister and I sat in the back on the old airplane seats my father had tied down for us and we had a canopy over us to keep the dirt from covering us. We wore scarves around our heads. Even so, we were covered with dirt whenever we arrived. Mother carried washcloths in a plastic bag. When we arrived at our destination, she would wash our faces and hands so we would be somewhat

presentable.

"She made a house a home," my dad used to say with a proud smile. My mom made all the curtains, bedspreads and home furnishings for our mud home. She was resourceful in creating things and even made all our clothes.

Letters took three weeks to get from where we lived in the jungle to the United States. People from our supporting churches wanted to send boxes. So, mom would give them a list of things they could send. They would send treats we couldn't get on the mission station. They sent chocolate chips for making chocolate chip cookies, cake mixes, and jello. Since it could take three months to get a box, by the time it arrived, it was stale. They were still delightful treats for us. We especially enjoyed making chocolate chip cookies.

Another special treat was Mom's homemade ice cream. She fixed a custard substance out of powdered milk. It was the only milk we could get. We didn't know the difference because we grew up with powdered milk. In those days, my mom had metal ice cube trays. She took out the insert and froze the custard mixture in the tray. We didn't know what USA ice cream tasted like. So, we thought Mom's makeshift ice cream was the best!

We had pets in Africa, especially cats, because they were good at catching mice. I had a special kitty that slept with me. She helped to ease my nighttime fears and comfort me.

Somehow, she got a fishhook in her mouth. This upset me to the point I cried hysterically, and my sister started crying too. My dad told us to go away. He tried to concentrate on getting the hook out of the cat, but we distracted and rattled him with our crying. Thankfully, he got the hook out and my mom put salve on the wound and covered it with gauze, and my kitty recovered.

We also had some unusual pets. "Look! We got another baby monkey!" My sister told me as she pointed to the baby monkey in the cage hanging outside our mud house.

The Africans would go into the jungle to hunt and kill monkeys to eat. Sometimes they killed a mother, so they brought the baby to us to nurture. My mother got a small cage to put the baby monkey in to protect it from predators and snakes.

My mother smiled at our joy and excitement. "We will need to feed the monkey with a dropper because it's too young to eat. You can take turns."

We took turns feeding the monkey using a dropper to drip milk into the baby monkey's mouth. Unfortunately, the baby monkeys didn't make it outside their home environment and without their mother. We even got an adorable chimpanzee we got to nurture for a period.

Another time when we were in the northeast part of Congo at Niangara, a small antelope wandered into our yard. It was lost, and the mother was not around. So, we cared for the little animal. We even got up in the night to feed it milk. One day, it wandered off into the

My sister, Kathi, interacts with the African children.

woods. We didn't see it again. These incidents taught us as children to care for animals and some unusual ones at that!

As children, we learned the African language and enjoyed interacting with the Africans, especially the girls, the children, and our caregivers. We would go into the village with supervision and visit the Africans in their mud huts. We were especially fond of some of the women who helped look after us and our household servants.

# Life in the Jungle (Part 2)

Friday night was our family night. "Sharon, get the fudge started, and I'll make the popcorn." Mom would tell me on Friday nights. I learned the fine art of making fudge to a perfect consistency and knew how long to beat it to get it nice and creamy.

We had little in the form of entertainment, so we created our own. Every Friday night we had a game night with games from the States. We popped popcorn and made fudge with the cocoa friends sent us. We had great fun on game nights with a lot of laughter. Sometimes the neighboring missionaries came over to play games with us.

Sandi and Sharon

We had a rich home life. When my mom married, she knew nothing about cooking or sewing. She wished her mother had taught her, but my grandma used to say, "Oh, it's easier to do it myself." So, my mother determined that her daughters would know how to cook and sew.

She taught us both skills. I remember the fun times in her bedroom where the sewing machine was set up. Sometimes she would make funny faces, especially if she made a mistake and my sister and I would laugh. We learned the joy of creating clothes from patterns. We took great pride in our creations.

When I was eleven years old, I followed a recipe by myself. I wanted to make a souffle since eggs were readily available. My mother tasted it, frowned, and spat it out. I followed the recipe. The only problem is that I put in 1 TB of pepper instead of 1 teaspoon! We had to throw it out. My mother never scolded me. She simply helped me understand what I did wrong so I could learn from my mistake. She taught me to develop a growth mentality.

This growth mentality is one I follow to this day. When I make mistakes, I ask myself, "What did I do that didn't work? What can I learn from this? What can I do differently in the future?" It's normal to feel bad about mistakes, but this has been a more constructive way to approach them.

One year, several months before Christmas, someone from the USA sent two big dolls. My mother hid them on the top shelf of the closet behind things to save them for us for Christmas. I don't remember how my sister and I found out, but we did. Frequently, my sister or I held the stool so the other one could climb up and look at the dolls. I don't remember getting the dolls for Christmas, but I remember the sense of adventure and mystery we created. We had more fun sneaking to see them than getting them.

Sharon, Kathi, Sandi with big dolls and makeshift Christmas tree.

My parents had to be innovative at Christmas. We didn't have access to the normal Christmas tree, so dad gathered branches and tied them together for a makeshift Christmas tree. Now that I look back on it, the "tree" was scraggly to say the least, but we didn't know the difference. As children, we thought it was amazing!

Though we had little, my mom liked to wrap a lot of little gifts for us to have. This way, we had a lot of gifts to open. Mom would take some of the extra little gifts and put them up for a later occasion. She reasoned we wouldn't play with so much in one day, and it would give her more to give us later. We never noticed.

Kathi, Sandi and Sharon with homemade
Christmas cookies to give.

When we were older, during the Christmas season, my sister, Sandi, Kathi, and I made cookies with my mom. We folded boxes out of red and green construction paper and put the cookies in the boxes. We then gave them to the Greek merchants and the Catholic priests in the small village town.

Christmas morning, we woke to Africans singing carols outside our windows at 5:00 a.m. Dad read the Christmas story to us, and then we opened our presents. Afterwards, we had church because for the Africans, Christmas was all about Christ's birthday. They would walk for an hour or longer to come to church and expect a 3 to 4-hour service. This was not only for Christmas, but every Sunday. The Africans

formed long lines to walk to church. You can't see it very well in the photo, but the line formed way beyond the palm trees. They were disappointed if the service was not a long one because they longed for spiritual nourishment from God's Word.

My mom home-schooled my sister and me in the elementary grades. You might think I'd be behind since we didn't have all the educational enrichment in Africa. Instead, when I returned to the USA during the 5th grade, I was a grade ahead in composition. In retrospect, since I love to write, this doesn't surprise me.

I used to even help my mother teach the African women how to read. They wanted to learn how to read so they could read the Bible and draw spiritual nourishment from it. She also taught the children

Mom teaching the children with flannel graph as Sharon watched.

using flannel graph figures to keep their attention.

When I was seven years old, my mother had my second baby sister, Kathi. I enjoyed helping my mother and taking care of her. I sat outside every day to sunbathe her for about 15 minutes. This way she could get vitamin D. This is a special memory to this day. She has a sweet spirit. When she was distressed, she always ran to me as her refuge.

Years later, my mother had another baby, Dianne, the fourth of us girls, when I was seventeen and my mom was thirty-eight. Since I was older, I cared for her all the time. I even got up in the middle of the night to feed her. I thoroughly enjoyed caring for her and watching her grow.

Not everything was idyllic. We had some challenges.

We had to wear helmets outside because of the scorching sun. For short periods, we were fine, but for any length of time, we had to be careful. We could get heatstroke.

Bath time for Kathi, Sharon and Sandi

We had to have all our water brought up from the river. Our servants would pour it in barrels that, in turn, came into the house. We had a wash basin with a pitcher of water. We had to boil all our water because it was very dangerous to drink it. Since the water was limited, the kids bathed together in a tub. Even with the precautions of boiling the water we drank, our dad got amoebic dysentery and almost died with it. Fortunately, he did survive but suffered for the rest of his life with repercussions from it.

Another challenge was all the bugs and pests. Some caused us to leave our home in the middle of the night!

# Driver Ant Invasion

At times in the middle of the night, my dad came into our rooms. "Get up girls and put on your shoes. Be careful. We have to get out of here because the driver ants are loose." We would have invasions of driver ants with pinchers on the top of their heads. We had to put on our shoes, stomp our feet vigorously, and run out of the house as fast as we could. We went to the neighboring missionary's house to sleep for the rest of the night. The driver ants would have killed us, similar to how they killed other trapped people and animals.

My mother wrote in one of her letters, "The driver ants are a menace and do have a painful bite. If they come into the house while you're sleeping, the small ones even come through the mosquito nets and start in on you. In a moment, you are up and have pinches. You must run for water and wash them off and get them off from crawling on your clothes. You must get out of the house until they get through eating everything." My mom described the results.

"Then they will clean out all the insects and rats mercilessly, killing any animal they can trap. In the forest, they have attacked and killed large animals. Even elephants flee before them and anteaters are overcome by their number. The thing to do is just not to get in a line of them. They can't kill humans unless they are helpless to run and except a baby who can't get away."

My mother continues to share about the driver ants. "One of our neighboring missionaries had the driver ants all over their yard and porch when they first came to the mission station. The ants went into the house, so they had to grab their things and go to the neighbors' house to sleep for the night." This had my mother worried about us, her daughters, as she describes.

"That is why we never dare to leave our big girls in the house alone at night for even a short time. Even if we go to another missionary's house, we get a babysitter. They really are no danger to us if we don't step in their line. We see them nearly every day and think absolutely nothing of it. We have all been bitten from time to time. It hurts and draws the blood but that's all. Fire drives them back and so does DDT."

She shared more about the driver ants. "They go in a line with the smaller workers on the inside and the big guards, which are half an inch long or more, on the outside, keeping them all in order. The bright sun will kill them, so they go into their house during the day or else through a dust tunnel over them as they march along. They are very interesting to watch. They spread out for attack and sometimes cover the whole road. You have to run quickly through them, or they will get in your shoes and under your stockings and pinch like crazy. The big ones just hurt really bad, and the little ones give you a jump."

My mother describes another time the ants took over. "One time, when Ernest was gone, we had them all over the porch three nights in a row. The third night we moved out because we thought they were going to come in the house."

I agree with my mom, the one good thing about when they came into the house, they would get rid of all the cockroaches in the house. Normally, it was quite disturbing to go into the kitchen in the morning and see all the cockroaches scatter. So, when the driver ants came, we had some reprieve from the cockroaches for a while.

The driver ants were not the only insect challenges we had. We had another bug that wanted to eat our home, literally!

# Termites, Pests and Diseases in the Jungle

We had a constant battle with various pests in the jungle. My mother writes about the dangers of termites, "We have a pesky ant that we call white ants. They are termites and very common in America, the book says. But those are not like here. These are an ever-present danger to all our possessions. They are always eating paper, books, cardboard, cloth, etc. We store songbooks or the African Bibles on a shelf in the attic or school supplies. We come back in a day or so and find them riddled.

"They can eat through a wooden box and destroy everything overnight. They can demolish a library just as quickly. They have come up through the floor and eaten a big hole in a chenille floor rug right off the floor. If you let the cupboard get pushed against the wall, it is very dangerous. They will smell it and come through the wall, through the cupboard, and eat up your sheets and whatever you have in the cupboard.

"We are careful and have lost very little but had some close calls. We got back from vacation, and they were eating the cardboard behind the bookcase. They were starting to build their nasty-smelling house onto the books, and soon many of the books would have been riddled.

"We've had several other close calls, such as the time all my precious Child Evangelism scenes were surrounded by them for two days in a row. I had spent hours, days, and weeks painting them and invested money as well. I sprayed them out, knocked down their house, and sunned the things only to have a repeat performance the next day. I keep them locked up in a metal suitcase now. All of our valuable things upstairs are stored in metal barrels with lids.

"One night, they attacked our neighbor's curtain in the living room. When she got up in the morning, she saw a rag on the floor riddled where the curtain had been the night before.

"They eat up the posts in a house and there is no way to know until the house falls down. The natives know, though, and they warn us. There is a house that we lived in at Ikozi, another mission station, that is absolutely full of them now and needs to be torn down. It is 8 years old, and 5 years is a good life for a mud house. Beyond that, they are not safe. There is no one in that one now, and they hope to tear it down and rebuild soon."

My mother continues in her letter to share other needs, "We have nine couples arriving on the field this year and so they need to build like crazy to be able to tuck them all in somewhere by next September. Things look like we'll be advancing in the next ten years. We sure need our doctor, hospital and a printer and equipment." She concluded her letter.

As I look back, I realize we had hardship by today's standards. At the time, these didn't bother me, since it was all I knew. For example, we had no light at night except for the generator. We had to use kerosene lanterns. We lit the wick and then carefully carried the lantern so we could see. Dad had a big one he would carry if we had to walk outside at night. But in our bedrooms, we had glass bulb lanterns.

When we went outside to the outhouse, we'd have to carry the larger lantern with us. We had to be careful not to step on any poisonous snakes. Anytime we walked to another missionary's house, we had to take a lantern with us and watch out for snakes.

The bugs were another issue. We had a variety of bugs, including large cockroaches. When we walked into the kitchen, the cockroaches scattered. We had to have mosquito nets on our beds to keep out the mosquitoes, bugs, and snakes. One time, when I woke up, there was a poisonous black mamba snake curled up on the top of my mosquito net. I hate to think about what would have happened if the mosquito net had not protected me.

We had jiggers that would burrow their way into our toes. So, we could not go barefoot outside. We had to always wear shoes. Even with shoes, these little fleas would get in our toes and form a white pus-like sack around them. The Africans were skilled at getting them out without breaking the sac. Otherwise, the infection would spread and cause serious problems. One of the biggest treats, when we came to the USA, was to take off our shoes and feel the grass on our bare feet.

My mother shares about the crickets. "We have crickets galore here by the forest, but they don't bother us. They are noisy at night, but I like it. They do eat the sashes of the girl's dresses sometimes as they hang in the closet.

"They don't annoy me as much as the giant size, inch-and-a-half to two-inch roaches swarming in and out of the house. They slip in from the forest and have babies in our house. They let out an odor like a skunk if they get annoyed.

"Fortunately, we have a dandy and beautiful cat, and it's a good ratter and even kills snakes. It also kills stink mice, and most cats run from them. The cat is protection for us. It killed a poisonous snake under the lounge where our African babysitter slept one night while we were next door."

We didn't have the flu. We had something more deadly, malaria. We had to take bitter-tasting quinine every day to kill malaria. Even so, we would get it from malaria-carrying mosquitoes. More than once, I can remember being deathly ill with malaria.

One time when I got malaria, I happened to be away at the boarding school in Kenya, which was a three-day drive from where we lived in Niangara, Congo. I was in the infirmary. I felt so alone and sick. I missed my mom so much!

We lived near a river, so our view was scenic. However, we also had to be aware of the deadly creatures in it. My parents did not allow us to go near the river because of the crocodiles. The Africans did all their bathing and washing of clothes in a river inlet where crocodiles don't normally go. They had to be constantly on the lookout in case a crocodile came. One woman ventured out too far, and the crocodile captured her. I can remember standing on the banks of the river with others sadly mourning her death as we held a service and sang.

Other dangerous creatures we had to watch out for were the hippos in the river. One night, we heard a ruckus outside our windows. My dad shone a flashlight into the eyes of a hippo. The next day we went outside to see that the hippos had trampled and eaten our plants and left large footprints. In the next chapter, I'll share a particularly scary story about a snake and our sister when she was a baby.

# Hero Cat

**M**y mother remarked to my sister and me, "What is the cat doing?" We sat playing on the slate floor of our mud house with a straw-thatched roof and whitewashed walls.

We had household servants who considered it a great privilege to work in our house. My mother trained them in household duties, but they were skilled in many other ways to serve and protect us.

One way we needed protection was from the snakes that were everywhere. During my mother's first month on the mission station, she reached down to get a magazine out of the magazine rack. She encountered a poisonous snake lying on the magazines! She screamed but got away before it harmed her. Needless to say, that was an unnerving experience!

We had to have mosquito nets over our beds at night because the mosquitoes carried malaria and other critters such as black mamba snakes.

Black mambas are the most feared and dangerous snakes in Africa. Their bites are venomous, and without an antidote, death is sure. The experienced servants stepped in to take care of the threat. We were grateful for their courage and their skill.

We had a good cat who kept the rat and mouse population under control. Now, my mother had observed the cat darting in and out of the playpen as my nine-month-old baby sister sat facing us. Her curiosity became aroused as she watched the strange behavior of the cat. She went over to look in the playpen.

When she bent over the playpen, she screamed and grabbed the baby out of the playpen. There, sitting behind my baby sister, was a deadly black mamba curled up inches away from her back.

"Girls! Girls! Get up on the couch. It's a snake!" We obediently dashed for the couch and jumped on it with my mother, who held the baby in her arms.

She continued to scream the word "Nzorka! Nzorka!" This meant snake in the native language. She yelled until one experienced servant raced in with a machete. He cut the head off the dangerous, poisonous black mamba.

The cat intuitively knew there was danger lurking in the playpen and wanted to warn us. If that cat had not been going in and out of the playpen, my baby sister might not have been saved and would not be with us now. The playpen was supposed to protect her, but snakes can get through the bars and apparently one decided that day to do so.

As I have reflected on this story, (Psalm 121:7, 8 NIV) comes to mind.

---

"The Lord will keep you from all harm—he will watch over your life.
The Lord will watch over your coming and going. both now and forevermore."

---

God has unusual ways of protecting us and that day He used a hero cat!

My mother faced many fears about going to Africa, but the Lord watched over her and her children. He watched over our coming and going and kept us safe from poisonous snakes and many other worse dangers.

If you feel God is leading you into something new, you may feel fear. I hope this will reassure you. He will watch over your coming and your going, both now and forevermore. So don't let your fears guide your decision. God is with you and will guide you into what He wants you to do.

# Hippo Chase and Other Dangers

**M**y sister and I heard my father yelling at us. "Run Sharon, run Sandi!" We were playing near the edge of a river when we visited a game park in Kenya. We had gotten out of the jeep and gone down near a river. We turned to see a large hippo with its mouth open rising out of the river a short way from where we played!

My father had seen the African guides stand and clap their hands as they took authority over the animals. They understood their God-given dominion and exercised it with confidence. We stood in awe as the animals responded and backed off.

Since my father observed this, he tried it. He clapped his hands to stop the hippo, but my father kept running as he clapped. We ran toward him as well. The hippo did not stop but kept charging. Fortunately, as we got closer to our African guide, he stepped in. He stood his ground, clapped his hands in authority, and the hippo turned and lumbered back to the river. What a relief!

I've used this in speeches as an illustration of what to do with our fears. When we face our fears and take a stand, they will flee.

In that game park, we got to see all kinds of animals in the wild, lions, giraffes, zebras, wildebeest, gazelles, and many more animals. When our jeep stopped, the monkeys jumped all over the vehicle and looked at us. We were not allowed to roll down the windows because they might grab us.

We had other dangers in our jungle home. We bathed at our house in tubs of river water that the household servants carried from the river. We had to boil it to drink it because of the disease potential. I can still see pots of water sitting around the house cooling. If we drank it without boiling it, we could become deathly ill.

Even with all the precautions, one time my father contracted amoebic dysentery and almost died. He might have contracted dysentery from one of his trips into the jungle. They had to drive him nine hours at 30 miles per hour over bumpy roads to Bukavu, the nearest hospital, to get help for him.

My mother homeschooled us when we were younger. She homeschooled me until the 4th grade before we

Mom homeschooled us when we were young.

went to the USA. Later when we returned from furlough in the USA, we went to Rethy Academy before we evacuated. My dad drove us to the boarding school 400 miles away from our mission station. Travel meant driving on deeply rutted roads at 20 or 30 miles an hour. When it rained, the roads turned red mud, and travel slowed down. Not only that, but the rain also often washed out the bridges. I can remember being stalled by a riverbank because the bridge had been washed out. Then we had to wait for a ferry to carry us across the river. Sometimes we got stuck in the mud, and my father and the Africans had to dig us out. In some places, the Africans had crafted what we called a "monkey bridge." These were bridges made from strong rope. The part you walked on was exceptionally narrow, so the bridge swayed high above the river. You

Dad in the middle of a monkey bridge.

had to hold on tight to the rope on each side to keep your balance. As a child, I thought it was fun, but as an adult, I'm not sure I would feel the same way!

When we drove by truck or car, usually a crude ferry operated by the Africans transported us across the river. However, if the river rose too high because of the rain, the ferry could not go.

Some of those swamp areas had high humidity. Those were the days before air conditioning, so we drove with the windows down. We wore scarves around our hair to keep the dust out. In some of those damp areas, we had to keep our windows rolled up

Sometimes we had to wait for a ferry because only one vehicle at a time could go across the river.

even in the stifling heat. My mom worried about sleeping sickness caused by the tsetse fly. If that fly bit us, we could become seriously ill and even die.

# Turmoil at the Border and Home

At that time in Africa, missionaries would go for five years. Then they would go on furlough to the USA to rest, regroup, and visit their supporting churches.

After we came back from the USA, our parents sent us to boarding school. We would go for three months and then go home to be with our parents for a month. It was harder on my mom than on me. She cried each time we left. Some kids had challenges because they had to be away from their parents. My younger sister was one of them. She hid in the closet when it came time to go. For me, it was fun to go to boarding school because I could see all my friends and we had a lot of activities.

Border barrier guarded with armed soldiers who threatened us.

At the end of our month off at home, my father drove us to the border of Uganda. Then a small airplane from Missionary Aviation Fellowship flew us to our school in Kenya, East Africa, called the Rift Valley Academy.

After the initial evacuation, we had constant challenges going to and from the border. The soldiers stopped us at the border before we could cross into Tanzania. Sometimes, my dad's hands shook, guns pointed at his back, as he pulled out the suitcases and laid them open on the ground.

The soldiers made us take out all our suitcases. They went through everything to make sure we weren't smuggling anything out of the country. They even opened the talking box on the back of a stuffed toy to see if anything was inside. We had to wait until they finished going through every item in the bags.

We often had barriers to stop us.

This could delay us for hours. They pulled out every little thing, even our underwear. Sometimes they pulled out feminine hygiene items. As teenage girls, watching men sift through our personal things embarrassed us. My mom said she didn't think they were worried about us smuggling as much as they were curious.

Different soldiers demanded different things. At one border, they even made dad take off the tire to see if there was anything hidden in there. My parents thought that was ridiculous, but dad had to comply. After all, the soldiers held guns.

One time, I noticed my father's hands shake more as he turned off the key in the truck. Even though the heat beat down on the cab of our truck, my father told my sister and me to stay in the truck. We were about fifteen and thirteen years old. He had heard stories of rapes of nuns and others, so he wanted to protect us. Teenage boys swarmed around our truck, raising their hands and jeering. Some pulled their hands across their throats as though they were going to slit our throats. I tried not to look at them as my sister and I sat there quietly. I'll never forget that scene. I can still see it in my mind. For some reason, I did not fear them. In my mind, my dad was with us. I had confidence he would protect us. Now, as an adult, I see how little power my dad had against the soldiers with their guns.

Sometimes, we had issues in addition to the border. The soldiers erected barriers on the roads we normally traveled. We had to pass through those to get where we were going.

After independence from the Belgians, the Africans had a lot of hostility toward the Belgians. At one barrier, the soldiers held their guns out and rushed at our car. My dad leaned his head out the window and yelled, "American. Protestant." Because the missionaries had helped the Africans in so many ways, the Americans had favor with the Africans. When the Africans lowered their guns and only checked our papers, we breathed a big sigh of relief.

For four years, these were the kinds of dangerous challenges we faced as they held us at gunpoint every time we drove to the border to go to school and back home.

Even going into town and back, the soldiers would stop you and fine you for every little thing. For example, mud on your license plate, which was ridiculous since all the roads were dirt, and when it rained, mud was abundant.

We weren't even safe in our homes. One time, two soldiers came to our house. My dad saw them, so he told my two sisters and me, "Go quickly and hide in the bathroom. Don't open the door!"

I later learned that the two soldiers made up some kind of paper that my father should have. My father told them, "We have all our papers," but the soldiers insisted, shifting their guns like they were threatening to shoot.

Sharon and Sandi handing out clothes to the African children.

My mother stood up to them. She reminded them of all the ways my parents cared for the African people, teaching them to read, giving them medicine and clothes, and many other things. "You don't want to shoot us because then who would do these things for your people?"

They lowered their guns, but they still demanded that my father give them money and then they would go away. With the lives of his wife and daughters at stake, my father complied and gave them money.

Mom used to say that these kinds of threats and demands for money happened more often at the end of the month because the corrupt government couldn't pay the soldiers. Somehow the soldiers needed to get money, so they made up these false charges.

# Fun at Boarding School

In my high school years, after the evacuation, I went to the Rift Valley Academy near Nairobi, Kenya. I participated in volleyball, basketball, soccer, high jumping, and cheerleading. Plus, I was in the choir and in the drama class. I even won a thespian award. Initially, I didn't make the cheerleading team because of the jumps. I didn't let that stop me. I was determined to improve, so I spent every moment practicing. I guess I must have overdone it because my grades slipped.

When we went home at the end of the semester, my dad teased me, "I have three daughters, one can read, one can write, and one can do cheerleading." At the time, his comments hurt my feelings. When I went back to school, my parents had my dorm mother put me at her dining room table in the evening. She supervised my studies.

I ended up making the cheerleading team as

Sharon loved cheerleading!

well as pulling my grades up. Because of the discipline, I graduated with high grades and went on to college, graduating on the honor roll. Now, in later years, I can see my dad didn't intend to hurt me, but rather he disciplined me because he loved me. As a parent, I understand his concerns. He disciplined me for my own good, and I am grateful.

Also, I learned that when I want something, not to give up if I fail. I learned to persevere in pursuing my heart's desire. When I didn't give up, I ended up achieving my heart's desire and made the cheerleading team. I had a lot of fun cheerleading too.

I had another opportunity to learn to persevere. I enjoyed high jumping. We had competitions at the school on certain days. On my own initiative, I went out day after day to practice. I knocked the bar over and over until I could finally scale it and move it up to the next level. I loved the challenge of competing against myself to improve.

This is a life principle that has helped me throughout my life. The goal is to challenge myself in whatever I'm doing to go to the next level of ability. For example, in my writing, I am at a far greater level than when I started. But I continue to learn, grow, and refine my skills.

When I was older, I went to boarding school. I loved boarding school. I missed my mom and dad, but I had friends and older girls I looked up to. We became family to each other. We ate together, played together, and went to school and church together. The younger ones went around to kiss the older ones goodnight.

My dorm mother made us feel special by having birthday parties in her suite. We could invite our roommates and a special friend or two. Miss Leitch made the difference for us. She was funny, kind, and understanding. She didn't put up with a lot of nonsense, but she was gracious in her discipline.

I loved the Rift Valley Academy with all the activities for us. They had team challenge sports. We had club days where we could take part in various hobbies. We could learn how to sew and cook and other skills. We even sewed our own cheerleading outfits.

RVA had a large choir, and we put on performances. Sometimes we would go to the large local city of Nairobi to perform. We had plays and drama opportunities. I won a thespian award in one play for successfully memorizing the most lines.

Ginger, Sharon, Sally, Sandi and Cathy in choir uniforms.

Despite all this fulfillment and joy, we had the turmoil of evacuation. When we traveled back home, we still had the threat of guns. In Congo, we lived in a state of constant vigilance. Amid all this, though, I found a safe haven at my schools, the Rethy Academy, and then later Rift Valley Academy. These were the best times of my life because I had challenges, goals, and friendships. I look back on my high school years as one of the happiest times of my life.

# Fascinating Letters from Africa

This next section contains letters my mother wrote to her father or mother or the churches who supported them in their mission. My mother had a fervent desire to care for the African people and others. She had a passion to share the Good News about Christ's gift of salvation with them. She also had a heart of compassion for those under her care.

Personally, her zeal, courage, and practical acts of love at such a young age fascinate me. She and my father were only in their mid-twenties when they went to the mission field. Yet, as you'll see later, the impact of their devotion, care, and the seeds they sowed continue to this day, over seventy years later. She and my father served God and cared for people with their whole hearts.

I trust you will enjoy these insights and experiences from the viewpoint of a missionary.

The first couple of letters were written from Belgium, where they spent a year learning French with my sister and me. Congo is about a third of the size of the United States, and yet every region had a different language. To give some context, imagine if you drove to the different states in the United States and each one had a different language. How would you

An air form letter sent from Africa. They used these blue forms because they were lightweight. Regular letters would be prohibitive in cost.

communicate? How would you trade goods and services? Yet in Congo, the regions were not even as big as a state. They had over 200 different languages; therefore, they needed a trade language. Because the Belgians colonized the Congo, French to this day is the trade language for "The Democratic Republic of Congo." This is the reason my parents needed to learn French. Later, they also learned the local African language for their region.

Some of my mother's accounts are routine but interesting to understand the everyday life of a missionary. Other accounts are fascinating in understanding cultural differences and life experiences in Africa. You can read straight through, as each letter is more or less a story in itself or skip to the ones you find interesting.

I tried to only edit for punctuation or clarity so you can get a sense of her personality, how she thought and wrote.

## Letters to Family
## May 9, 1952

This letter was written from Brussels, Belgium, to her father.

How can I thank you enough? The things have all arrived, and we are so very, very thrilled with all of them. The girls (my sister Sandi and me) are so thrilled too! Cinderella is even in that book and the games came today.

I'm going to buy a little souvenir from every place we go. Our ship stops in Spain, Italy, Egypt, Suez Canal and more. We are planning a trip through Germany to Switzerland for a much needed rest when all the French courses are finished. We are saving for that trip now. Ernest will probably be worn out. The French courses coming up are sooooo hard and all day long. They are very hard for the Belgians, let alone a stranger, to pass. They are all in French, of course. We get along pretty well in French now.

If you ever sell a house and want to do something wonderful, I have prayed for several years for something special. I hesitate to say anything but have wanted to for so long. Ignore it if you think I shouldn't ask. Juanita (her sister, also a missionary), is so talented, and an accordion is just the instrument for the mission field. She has longed for one of the lightweight 120 bass ones for so long. I saw one advertised in the Sears catalog for only $169.95. It sounds like a good one and only weighs 12 lbs. I sure wish she could have one. Ernest would have bought me a used one once, but I don't have the talent for it. They are such an aid on the field or any Christian work.

## Thanks for the Financial Help

August 27, 1952

Dear Daddy,

What a wonderful time we've been having! Thank you so much daddy for your gift. After you've done so much to get Juanita (her sister) financed for nurses' training, I did not see how you could send money to us, too. I had not expected anything. I was so glad you could do it for my sweet little sis.

We needed the money more than I realized. We found out that our passage fund (the ship fare to Africa) is quite a bit shorter than we realized. We hope to save your check as much as possible for that trip. We have drawn from our equipment and passage fund for shoes into the future of the sizes the children will be needing, socks, underwear, two dresses, hand-me-downs, a belt for Ernest and various things like that. I think we have enough to get us to the field with your money only lacking about $100 or so, maybe $200. We sent out a prayer letter about it and I think it will come in okay. I pray you will sell enough to pay you back rich.

## Family Life

April 20, 1953

Dear Family,

Sandra is so big. She's plump and rosy-cheeked and always laughing and saying great big words. We sure do enjoy our children. They play Old Maid with us now and it's a lot of fun. Sharon is quite a whiz, too. She asks questions all day long and some are just without answers. "Why do we breathe?" "Where does the rain come from?" "What makes night?"

Her school supplies have arrived, and we are eagerly anticipating starting. I haven't had the time now as we are studying hard to get the language quickly. We work all day and every evening on many things we have to do, but we are going to stop and take our evenings sometimes for reading and recreation. We'll become stale if we don't. Besides, one sure needs some time out. We're drivers, I'm afraid, but we do feel conscientious about the job God has called us to do. We have to go to bed at 9:00 p.m. and lay down a little in the afternoon as we get up fairly early and in these tropical climates, you need more sleep. If you stay up too many nights in a row, you'll wake up with malaria. I don't like to go to bed early, but Ernie does, so he is good for me.

I want to put some of Sharon's lovely colorings at age four in your card and then you could give them to grandmother because she loves to save things like that we have done. She told me that she still has a lot of my baby things and pictures. She has planned it, so we all get them when she passes away.

You would be quite thrilled to hear Sharon and Sandra rattling off French. Sharon says connected sentences and understands much of what is said to her.

You cannot imagine the darkness those who don't know the Lord live in. The devil's power is certainly manifested where he is worshiped. It takes a long time and much training on our part, much patience, and prayer to develop people from such a background into strong Christian leaders. It is worth it all, though.

~~~

**Note from the author**: My mother wrote the following letter to a church that supported them. These are what missionaries call "prayer letters." The letters share the triumphs and the need for prayers. As a fair warning, she is full of zeal and evangelistic in her prayer letters. To me, her passion and fervor are admirable.

~~~

# French Exams and Exciting Decisions for Christ

E rnest passed the French exams!!! European examinations are very different and much harder than any we have yet heard of in the States.

"The effectual fervent prayers of a righteous man availeth much." (spiritual power) (James 5:16 KJV) How we thank you for your intercessory prayers! We really needed them! Everyone was so worn out that when the exams were over, several had to go to bed and stay awhile.

The professor was quite pleased with Ernest's progress and complimented him on his work.

This year has been a valuable one. These materials will be essential to our work in Congo, and we are so thankful for the French we have learned. Sharon speaks fluent French with a Belgian accent now. They tell us you could never tell she was an American by her accent.

Three souls for him in Belgium! We were told, "Only those who must have souls will have them." We decided we must have them! The first answer to this prayer was Sharon's school teacher who accepted Christ. She witnessed right away to her parents and was reading her New Testament and memorized some verses. She was only permitted to return once for Bible study. Pray that this young woman will grow in the Lord and to be a witness among her many friends and that we might have further contact here.

We met a worldly young man soon after and had him over one night. Our assistant pastor was here. We had a long and heated conversation. The young man was quite intelligent but denied the existence of God and the truth of the Bible. However, the evening made a tremendous impression on him.

He read a booklet that we gave him and his New Testament and accepted Jesus a few days afterward. He has changed tremendously and comes regularly for Bible study, manifesting a hunger for the Word of God. He has witnessed to others a lot and had to leave home for a while because of his stand for Christ before his socialist parents. Pray for him to withstand the many temptations.

He brought his girlfriend to us and before the evening was over, she too accepted Christ. Her face lit up with joy, and it was wonderful to behold. She wanted victory in her life and was especially happy to know that God would answer her prayers now. She has struggled but has had victory in several respects. The

Lord did all this with our poor French! Friend, have you asked Him for souls this month? "Ask and ye shall receive that your joy may be full" (John 16:24 KJV).

An eighteen-year-old is suffering much persecution for accepting Christ. She went to a Billy Graham crusade when she visited her sister in America. She grew a lot in the Lord during her year in the United States. We met her at the Maranatha Bible Camp last summer.

Her communist father and mother were very angry to hear their daughter had accepted Christ. Her persecution in the home had been severe. Though she lives in a large city in France, she couldn't find other Christians. For eight months, she searched and prayed for some kind of Christan fellowship. The only thing she had was frequent opportunities to pick up the "Back to the Bible Broadcast." This has sustained her during this difficult time. She had met Brother Epp and enjoyed his ministry at a camp in America.

After we were in Belgium, we sent her an invitation to come visit. Our letter came just as she had been praying earnestly for fellowship with someone here in Europe who knew Christ. Her parents reluctantly permitted her to stay with us for three weeks. We were very crowded in our three rooms, but she helped us with our French, and we helped her.

She heard the gospel for the first time in her French, her native tongue. She learned her first French hymns, scripture verse, and gave her first public testimony before a large group of people. They were very challenged by her testimony. They asked her many questions about America and the revivals there. They can hardly believe it because gospel work is so slow and hard here. She returned with the desire to be a missionary nurse to her own people in France.

We had the opportunity to visit twice at length with a Belgian official who works with the Congo languages. He and his wife are such wonderful people, and we desire to reach them with the gospel. There are others. Please continue to pray. Your prayers sustain us when the going gets rough.

~~~

**Note from the author:** The following letter was written from Ikozi, Bukavu, Belgian Congo (now the Democratic Republic of Congo) Africa before my parents went to their permanent mission station assignment at Kamulila. This is a prayer letter to the churches who supported them in the USA.

# Encouraging Response June 1953

**D**ear Co-laborers in the work of the Lord in Congo,

The drums beat excitedly, calling the people to greet us at a little village beside the path. We have just returned from our FIRST evangelistic trip in Congo. Heavy rains had caused the roads to be blocked, so we were glad to spend the night with a fine young native preacher who had been trained at our Katanti station.

After supper, people thronged into his little mud hut. Seated around the lamp, they listened to the gospel records in their own language. One man said, "You white men have great wisdom to make phonographs and airplanes. You are like God." We denied this and spoke to him of all wisdom, being in God and coming from Him.

Then our fine elder preached to them about the wisdom that we had come to share with them, which is found in His book, the Bible, the way of salvation through our Lord Jesus Christ.

There was a Christian Chief in the district who came to the meeting. There were many men present wearing only loin clothes of pounded bark cloth. I talked with one nice old Christian woman who had borne 10 children and lost all but two. Her husband had other wives as well. She and several others begged us to have another service in the morning, which we consented to do. We slept for the first time in a native house. We're glad for our mosquito nets as there were other living creatures crawling about all night.

We had a large group with several tribes represented, gathered under the stairs, waiting for us at our destination the next evening. There were two drum calls that night. One to the heathen dances, which take place every moonlit night in the villages nearby, and another call to the regional meeting of all our villages and native preachers in that large mining area. (Drums were the way the Africans communicated messages to others not close to their village. Different beats communicated certain messages.)

After our meeting with them, we were glad to see our cots set up in the teacher's tiny bedroom.

The next morning, the little church was brightly decorated with flowers and palms from the forest. It was crowded beyond capacity, with people peering in at every window and door. We enjoyed speaking to them in their own native language, though we are by no means fluent yet.

Please continue to pray for us with respect to the language. The tones are so hard to incorporate into everyday speech and yet they are of vital importance. Many words are spelled exactly the same, the only difference being the tones. For instance, if we use the wrong tone, we say that Jesus has washed our sins away with his tales instead of His blood. Natives on the mission station understand us, but what must the average unbeliever in the village believe when we make such blunders?

A young Belgian saved through the influence of missionaries while we were in Belgium has come to the Congo for the express purpose of reaching Africans for Christ while working in one of the mines. It is very difficult for a Protestant to raise support in Belgium. He has only been here two months, but the whole tribe already knows that a good master, a Christian, who lives and believes like the missionaries, has come to work in the mines. He holds the advantageous position of the personnel manager.

He arranged a meeting for us in the native clubhouse in this community of about 1000 native workers. The natives preach to the different tribes in three languages, and we spoke in Kilega. Our Belgian friend is continuing his Bible studies by correspondence from the Belgium Gospel Mission and hopes to enroll in Moody's Bible correspondence course soon. Pray for him as he learns the language and ministers in that meeting place.

We had six meetings in all over the week and three people made professions of faith in Christ. Two backsliders came back to the Lord. One man lost his wife and child. He wanted to kill the man he suspected of poisoning them, but changed his mind at the meeting.

By now, we have plenty of snake stories to tell. Last week I picked up a wicker table with a deadly poison viper crawling on the under ledge. I was holding it tightly in my hand. This made it very angry and ready to strike. I threw it to the floor and the household servants rushed in and killed it.

This reminds me of this verse. "Are not his angels all ministering spirits sent forth to minister to them who shall be heirs of salvation." (Hebrews 1:14 KVJ).

In response to Mrs. Amiee's (missionary on our station) daily Bible classes, there has been the beginnings of a Revival in our midst. One Sunday, several of our Christians yielded their lives to the Lord at the morning service and three of my household servants were among them.

One is a very intelligent boy in quite a high clan of the tribe. He is therefore given to pride and a bad attitude sometimes. We need leaders of his caliber, but he has many spiritual lessons to learn before he can be used. I talked with him at length one night and prayed for him. He thanked me and prayed that the Lord would help us to train him from the Word in the way that he should walk and enable him to be victorious over his old sin nature in the strength of Jesus Christ.

He has been very different since, though he still has his ups and downs. We told you of the salvation of his wife in our last letter. Now they have a new baby. It was our privilege to furnish clothes and a blanket. Pray for them.

Pray for us for the Lord's choice of household servants for us at Kamulila. They are mostly uneducated people from the jungle. Therefore, it's difficult to find ones that will catch on and fit in. Our mud house will not be finished until July or August.

The Christians there labor against the powers of darkness. You will be glad to know that many who have gone away to the Catholic schools are returning. We learned that Kubali had been spoken to fervently by our head servant but had never accepted Christ.

~~~

**Note from the author:** Some may be curious about the mud houses. Our mud house was a square house with slate floors. We had two bedrooms, a kitchen, a living room and a bathroom. The African mud huts were round with dirt floors. We had the same thatched roof that the African houses had. The mud kept the houses cooler during the extreme heat of the day. Back then, we didn't have the option of air conditioning. The mission compound existed in a clearing next to the jungle and was subjected to the unrelenting heat of the sun. However, because of the house construction, we were not uncomfortable in the house.

Mom, Sandi and I visited a mud hut of an African friend.

# Evangelistic Trip Into the Unknown July 1953

Evangelistic trip–this letter was written by my dad. This is a rare gem since he did not write much.

~~~

I had the privilege of going with two other missionaries and three native teachers on an evangelistic trip to a tribe north of here. This is the only gospel witness in the whole southern part of the tribe. It was a real joy to tell them of our Lord and Savior, Jesus Christ, and His great love for them. Many were very attentive and asked questions. None made a decision to take Christ as their Savior, but the Word of God was sown in their hearts. We are asking the Lord for a reaping of the seeds sown there soon.

Our mission is planning to open a station there as soon as the state grants us permission. Some people have the idea that they should not accept Christ until we have a mission up there. Pray with us that the Lord will so work in their hearts that some will accept Christ now before they die and go to a Christ-less eternity. We have been working among them and are asking the Lord to give us the faith to believe in Him for the work which He is going to do.

We will be moving to Kamulila sometime in August when our mud house is finished. They have to make the doors and the windows and lay the rock floors yet. The Africans there are eager to have us come, and we are anxious to go. I will be directing the school there as well as teaching some to read, including the Bible and French. Pray with us that the Lord will use His Word to bring forth fruit in the schoolboys' lives and the women.

I will need much prayer as I haven't taught before and I've only been studying Kilega, their native language, for eight months. We know we're not sufficient of ourselves, so our sufficiency will have to be of God. Pray with us as we move so that we might start in the right way with these people.

We want to evangelize the people in the villages as well as those on the mission station. In order to extend out evangelistic efforts and for emergencies, we need some form of transportation. We have an opportunity to buy a 1950 1/2 ton pickup truck in good condition for $1000 if the funds become available.

While we were at Katanti, an expectant mother was brought in near death. Our nurse worked all night trying to save her. Then we took her to the hospital at

Shabunda. She died a short time later. The pitiful death wail of her husband is one of those who has no hope of seeing their loved ones again. (Wailing was customary among the Africans in response to death. When someone died, they would surround the dead person, throw themselves on the ground and wail for three days.)

This is why we're here to share the good news of Jesus Christ's sacrifice and the hope of heaven when someone dies.

While I was at the hospital, Virginia was at a village meeting where four village girls made professions of faith in Christ. This is the hope we bring them.

**Note from the author:** In the jungle where we lived, the Africans believed in the supernatural and feared the powers of darkness. Many of them sought witchdoctors for health remedies, to put curses on people and other things.

Once they believed in and accepted Christ, they were set free from participation in and fear of those dark forces. My parents taught them that as Christians, we don't need to fear Satan or demonic forces. We are more than conquerors through Christ and greater is He who is in us than he who is in the world. Jesus has given us authority over all the power of the enemy and all evil forces. (Romans 8:37, I John 4:4, and Luke

10:9, NKJV) Those who have been taken captive can be set free.

In this next chapter, I'm sharing a letter my mother wrote to her dad in which she shares stories of a couple of African women who were set free.

# Just Call Me Nurse – Miraculous Healing and Deliverance
## December 4, 1953

Dearest Daddy,

Every week when the runner goes up to the gold mine to meet the weekly mail truck, I have intended to send a letter. Somehow we have a time getting letters written because it's one thing you can put off.

Last week, Betty, the nurse and her husband Irving, had to be away on business. So, Iola, the single woman, who is living with them until her house is finished, kept their children. The three of us are the only white folks around here. We were hoping no medical emergencies would arise in Betty's absence. There is an Italian doctor at the mine. It's not close, but we could take someone there.

Well just call me, nurse. In Betty's absence, we had plenty of emergencies! Iola and I pitched in with the help of our well-trained capable native nurses. All are male except for one mid-wife helper for deliveries. We delivered three babies.

One woman almost died, and we were going to take her to the doctor, but after our native nurse shot her with penicillin and a heart stimulant, she came around. While we were getting the car ready to go, she suddenly delivered. She had a convulsion that lasted for one hour with her eyes fixed. She was not hearing or answering, teeth clenched, heart beating fast and irregular, but the medicine brought her around.

She began calling for the witch doctor and native medicines and refused to go to the doctor. However, her relatives wanted us to go. Sometimes the relatives refuse and let them die but this man said, "She cost me a lot of money (dowry). It would cost me a lot to buy another wife. Take her to the doctor. We can see she is dying."

She had four children already. We prayed and the Lord worked a real miracle and healed her without a trip to the doctor, and in spite of our ignorance, she delivered a strong baby boy. She had more convulsions, but responded immediately to another heart stimulant. It had been four hours since the last stimulant. Afterward, she said, "Pray again and thank God." She realized how close she had been to death, and she admitted that only the Lord had saved her life. She said in her language, "Jesus Christ is God very truly! "After she listened to the plan of salvation which she had heard already, she prayed with me to accept Jesus as her Savior.

Betty says down here in the jungle, quite often a medical case of convulsions instead turns out to be demon possession, especially if they practice witchcraft. If they accept Christ and sever those relationships, the convulsions never reoccur.

The wife of one of our leading evangelists at Kantati was badly possessed by demons. Two nights in a row, before she was saved and before she married, she was in the girls' home. She had to be held down in bed by several big girls because she kept screaming that she wanted to go into the forest and dance with the spirits. Had she gone, she would never have returned because the wild beasts would have gotten her at night when she was alone in the forest.

When she came to, they dealt with her, and she accepted Christ and got free of the demonic forces. That was years ago and now she's married to one of the finest native preachers in the area. They have three lovely children, and she has a real zeal for the Lord.

Ernest has had many successful weekend trips, visiting other villages or going into the jungle, lately. We girls manned the station alone last weekend, deliveries and all the other things that come up on the mission stattion.

Fortunately, I can drive if I have to, but I sure don't do it much on these roads with tiny ferries that to go over the fast-moving rivers.

Also, these roads are just winding mountain trails through forested jungles.

# Enthusiastic Response
## Prayer Letter October 1952

O n September 11th, the old '38 Ford truck bounced up the road to the village of Kamulila, loaded beyond capacity with our belongings. People rushed forward from everywhere, clapping their hands and shouting to greet their long-awaited missionaries. They sang to welcome us.

We started school almost immediately, with a day of prayer and a week of evangelistic meetings during the Bible hour. Lutete, our fine young native evangelist, preached each morning from the Gospel of John. Nineteen boys made professions of faith in Christ during the week. One came to the mission to become one of our preacher/teachers in the out villages.

Each month, we have a regional conference at a village in the surrounding territory. At our last one, 37 villages were represented. People walked miles and some for days to attend. The meetings often lasted three or four hours, but even the children paid close attention.

A sub-chief, who is over five villages, accepted the Lord after Irving Lindquist, (another missionary on the mission station) talked to him at length. The next day, he brought another sub-chief. If this man comes out for the Lord, he can be a big influence on the people. Smoking and drinking have a strong hold on him. Pray for his deliverance. Five other professions of faith were made at the meeting. The teachers and native evangelists in outlying villages need your prayers because they stand alone in very difficult places.

Because there are several unsaved workmen and their wives on the mission station, we had evangelistic meetings last week. We were rained out for two nights. Two of the workmen, one woman and one girl, accepted the Lord. The little girl's father had died, and she said, "I want to accept the Lord because something could happen to me too."

Ernest supervises the schools and teaches several classes a day. He also has evangelistic work and all the out-stations and teachers. I teach Sharon and Tommy Lindquist (child of another missionary) in school each morning and will work with the African women and the school for the girls. Working with the women can be discouraging as they are less willing to learn. Many never learn to read. Pray for our work with them.

Your missionaries in Congo,
Ernest, Virginia, Sharon and Sandra

# Rainy Climate September 1954

Dear Daddy,

You asked about the climate. There isn't too much to say about it. It's always so much the same. It rains and rains and rains! We have a long rainy season. We're only 4 degrees from the equator in the densely forested, mountainous section, so it rains all the time from September to May, except for a short semi-dry season in January.

The mountains spare us the dense heat we'd otherwise have to endure. The sun is terrific, but we are cool in our mud houses or in the shade. We've had days where it rained all day and all night, drizzling and storming. Then it gets so cold and muddy. The red mud is like clay and gets tracked all over the house. The servants sweep once or twice a day and even then, it's sometimes futile. The climate here is very damp. We have a hard time keeping film because it is to be kept in a cool dry place. Here if it's cool, it's wet. If it's hot, it's dry. The attic is dry and hot because of the sun.

Some chickens built their nests in our roof and made a nice hole in it. We knew it was some kind of animal up there bigger than a rat and our cat didn't seem to be the guilty one. Ernie was in school so when I heard the noise this morning, I climbed up there "bravely" I might say. Our fears turned to laughter when we discovered the guilty but two persistent mother hens. We had fresh leaves put on and blocked it.

Then during our dry season, July-August, it's our winter since it's a little cooler, but not much. It still rains frequently but our streams dry up some and it's hard to get enough drinking water and other clean water for cooking, kitchen, laundry, and bathing. If it didn't rain some, we'd have trouble surviving because we'd run out of water. There's always the filthy Ulindi River water close here, but it's no good except for toilet flushing and then it plugs up the pipe in from the barrel. So, we don't use the barrels, we just flush with the buckets of dirty water.

Otherwise, we have gasoline barrels (two outside the bathroom; one for the toilet and one for the sink) where we wash our hands and one outside the kitchen over the sink. The servants keep those filled up, and it's piped into the house. It's very handy. We have a shower rigged up. A barrel upstairs is filled by the servants with warm water, and it has a shower attachment that hangs into that area.

We had a nice shower thing built out of cement, and we painted it white, and we have a nice plastic curtain I bought in the USA. We bathe the girls in a metal tub inside the shower area.

You should see the servants swinging their hips in rhythm as they carry a pole over their shoulder with a bucket full of water on each end. Picture a tall slim boy in a ragged shirt just about falling off, swinging down the path, a pole slung over his shoulder with leaves laid over the top to keep the water from splashing out as he walks. They amaze me because they are so sure-footed.

## Ernest Gets Very Sick with Malaria

Back to the climate. We never have heat like your summers, though. This is a mountainous region and has a lovely climate. The sun is so hot though that even through a hat, you can get sunstroke if you are out all day. You would be sure to get malaria if you were in all the sun all day.

We wear sun helmets, but the only time it's ever really gotten to us was when Ernest tramped all day in the forest going to villages to preach. The sun didn't seem like much in there, but it was such a hot, close, damp heat and he was so worn out that he was really sick for three days.

But Bikugi, our cook and head servant and Lutete, our head elder and evangelist (Ernest's right arm sometimes) were there. They took such loving, good care of him and got up in the night and sat by him and prayed for him. They just wouldn't leave him. They wanted to send a runner for a doctor and carry Ernest to the road, but he was too sick to go. Anyway, he knew it was just malaria, and he had all the medicines he needed for it with him. He knew the only thing to do was to take the medicine and sweat it out in bed until it was finished. He got better and was able to go on, but he sure did take the kipoi.

The kipoi is like a hammock seat with poles on the end and not too comfortable. Four Africans each carry one of the poles in rhythm. The first day he thought it was just as comfortable to walk as to ride in the kipoi, but after he got sick, he rode in it except for when they had to go straight up and down the mountain.

Some places, it was so steep that one man pulled Ernest by the hand in front, and another pushed behind so he could make it straight up and over the ridges and rocks. The Africans never slip because they dig in with their toes. But while Ernest is surefooted, he had shoes on too and that didn't help matters any.

While the sun's rays penetrate and damage if one is out for long periods of time without a good sun helmet, we're now so used to it that we can take a lot more of it than we could to begin with. We don't have to wear a helmet except in the hot parts of the day. The kids can take more tan as they're always in it and playing. They hate to keep a helmet on. I used to battle that issue all day, but now they play in the shade when it's too hot and otherwise they and the other missionary kids seem to take it more and adjust better than the adults do.

In the house, it's nice and cool. We sleep under three quilts every night. I keep the children in lightweight flannel pajamas because they get uncovered even though they sleep under a blanket. It's very cool sometimes in the morning during the rains and after sunset. The sun sets at 6. It just all of a sudden drops and night just falls. It seems to go down fast in Africa, and we don't have much twilight.

The nights are lovely. The animals and birds call strangely and beautifully from the forest and in the bright full moon one can see palm trees outlined against the sky. You can hear the Africans singing hymns in their native language around their campfires and playing games. In the distance, sometimes the drums call the villagers to a night of dancing in the moonlight. It's all part of Africa.

We'll miss the sounds in the night when we leave the peace and quiet of the jungle for the fast-paced turmoil of America, the busses passing, the horns honking, cars racing, the neighbor's radio blaring. All the same, I'd love to come home for a while.

We'd like to settle down in Wichita and put the kids in school and I'd go to PTA (Parent Teacher Association) and be a normal American mother. I'd like to take some art lessons at the museum if there's time and maybe sit in on a few nights or day courses at the university. But we'll probably have too many meetings where we need to speak.

There are always a lot of deputation meetings. (meetings where churches invite you to share about your mission work to raise support) People want you from California to Washington, D.C. All the same, if mother is there, she can take care of the older girls, and we can give them one year of normal American school life. I'll take the baby with me and try to be home with the girls as often as we can.

# Treats in Bukavu and Family News

## February 27, 1954-Letter to Family

We went to Bukavu recently. (Bukavu was the nearest large city) I hadn't been for 15 months, 1 year and 3 months! I really was anxious to go after so long in the bush (the jungle). You know how well I like to shop and go places. I'm not a stay-at-home type and it's not easy to settle down and sit with no place to go and no one to see all the time. I'm getting used to it and we keep busy, so I don't notice it too much, but I was beginning to insist that we go to town. I love to shop, and I could not wait any longer. After two months or so of saying I was going to Bukavu if I had to walk, I talked Ernest into getting a substitute to teach his classes so we could go.

Ernest had an evangelistic trip on the way, halfway there, so we all went. There were 25 conversions in 3 days in six villages, and one was a chief. His wife had just died, and we said, "If it had been you, where would you be now?" He accepted Christ the next morning.

We enjoyed Bukavu, and I splurged on some treats we hadn't seen for years, dates, cream cheese, etc. We had delicious ice cream cones with several missionary friends in and around Bukavu. I found several bargains in case lots, so we did save some, although the trip cost a fortune. Bukavu is 150 miles away, and it takes 9 hours. We average 15 miles an hour with all the curves and narrow mountain trails through the forest with mountains all along the way.

Gas costs 75 cents a gallon and we only get a few miles to a gallon, so gas alone comes to about $40. The mud roads were rough and bumpy. We had four flats and finally had to buy a new tire for the car.

We had a grand time. I found some canned peaches from home (USA), a 22 cent can marked 76 cents, but I didn't care. I wanted some peaches, so we bought them. The kids got some bubble gum. We really splurged. We had been saving for months, so it worked out.

## Sharon's Care for
## Sandra's Salvation

February 27, 1954

Finally, Ernest said I could order a nylon dress. It will be so nice when we travel. I've wanted one for so long and everyone else I know has one. On the ship, I was out of place in the dining hall in the evenings. Several had on formals; all were dressed up really nice. I'd given away all my rayons as the bugs eat them so badly here, so I only had cottons to wear. Next time, I can dress up too.

Sharon put her arm around Sandra and had her sit down and taught her more about Christ as she went into great detail and then prayed with her. Sandra said she accepted Christ as her Savior because "He died for my sins on the cross. I am a sinner and want His blood to wash away my sins."

Bless her heart. She's not quite four, but Sharon was saved a little younger than this and has meant business about it ever since. She is sincere.

## Tea Set, Entertaining and Personal Needs

March 16, 1954

Dear Daddy,

Mother said the mission was so busy they did not get around to sending things for a while. I was sorry to hear that because some things I've been wanting to get for quite a while are out of stock such as the tea set.

It is customary when Europeans drop in and even often with other guests to serve afternoon tea and cookies. I have nothing for that but just use my company cups and our kitchen tea pot. I looked all over in Belgium and England, but the tea items were too expensive. Finally, I decided to go ahead and order this lovely one from Wards catalog.

I also need the flannel which I must have for my child evangelism work to make scenes. I'm nearly out, so I hope that came through.

I'm disappointed that they didn't have or send the dark slip I ordered with that sheer nylon dress. I can't wear it with a white one very well and I wanted it for the conference and vacation time. I just don't have any good dresses left after 2 1/2 years away from home. I have everyday dresses because I'm little and everyone sends me nice hand-me-downs for every day.

We have to borrow two cots for the children every time we go out into the villages together, which is at least once a month, so I do hope they sent the cot. I'm going to try to get another from one of the missionaries going home to the US as we need four. The children are getting too big to sleep together. They kick each other all night on one cot and wake up crying. It's hard to be so far from a store like this. I hate to impose on others all the time, but we just have no choice.

# Birthday Party and Witchcraft Charms

March 20, 1954

Dear Daddy,

We had a nice little birthday party for Sharon's and my birthdays. (I was born close to her birthday) I taught school as usual but, in the evening, we had a hot dog roast. The native boys asked, "Do all the people in the foreign country eat outdoors on the day of their birth?"

They don't have birthdays since they never counted the days and years before missionaries came. I made some hot dog buns and a nice sponge cake. I've learned to cook so much more since we came out here because there is so much that we can't buy, and we can't get mixes. I can even make cheese crackers to eat with soup. We like crackers so well that I was glad to find a recipe.

We have some very interesting animal bags of witchcraft charms to show you when we come home. Some Africans have gotten convicted about it and have given them up after salvation and gave them to us. (Later, we had to destroy these because of their evil attachments, and they weren't safe to keep).

We were talking the other day and Sharon said, "When I go home and see granddaddy, I'll crawl up on his lap and he'll give me pennies out of his pocket again." I was surprised she seemed to remember. I thought you would be pleased.

## Kitchen Dishes and Shirts for Men

September 20, 1954

Dear Daddy,

Thanks so much for the aluminum glasses and bowls. I surely do need them. Out here, our servants break the breakable ones as fast as you buy them, or the kids break them on these slate floors. The only ones we can buy cost 25 cents each for ordinary glasses. My plastic ones have been valuable to me after four years of use and two of those in Congo, they're beginning to peel, and one sprung a leak. Also, I need bowls. My good set of dishes has no bowls for soup or porridge and when we had company, we had to use every size and sort of bowl until we found some plastic ones in Bukavu at 30 cents each. But they were plastic and most of them are cracked or broken now. The pitchers will be nice for fruit juice and milk. Of course, our milk doesn't come in a bottle like there. We can't drink water out of the faucet, so we use pitchers a lot. Thanks for everything!

I bet you forgot to include some of your old shirts. If you ever happen to send another box, remember how the Africans need used clothes and sweaters you're not using. They would be delighted, and so would we be as we constantly try to dig up something for our servants, elders and teachers and the schoolboys to wear.

Folks at home discard a shirt with a frayed collar, a patch or a scorch, but here it's worn to Sunday as their "best." Jim (brother-in-law) sent a bunch that we thought were too good to discard and Ernest was even wearing some of them. I suppose they were too small for Jim. He sent us a lovely set of used Compton's encyclopedias and my how we use them! I use them all the time with the children and for the Africans. I'm so glad that he is interested in our work too and in us, because that makes it easier for Juanita (her sister) and me to go on being the pals we've always been. She's still my very best girlfriend and I am hers, too.

# Dangerous Animals, Africans Protect Virginia

A man was killed near here by a wild buffalo the other day. He arrived here at the dispensary but died as he got here. He was out hunting but not well armed.

There was a gorilla in a village where we had slept when we went on the mission trip into the forest. A man tried to drive the gorilla out of his garden or tried to and got his nose pulled off by the gorilla.

In the forest trip, Ernest saw elephant and gorilla tracks and heard their calls. Also, there are wild pigs, antelopes and not too far, occasionally, a leopard. But right here where we are, we don't have those animals close because we have too many villages and clearings.

The Africans walk alone, fearless in this section and sometimes without lights. We never fear the animals, but when I've gone out for a little walk at night, the Africans come running after me, insisting on making sure nothing happens to me. One night I saw a group of girls from our girls' home following me and later I saw one of our elders. I asked them what they wanted, and they said, "We saw you go out walking and were worried about you, so we decided to follow you to protect you."

The elder said, "I didn't see the girls, I just saw you go and didn't know who else to send so I dropped everything and came myself to take care of you in case an animal would come." I laughed but agreed that if they were worried, then they knew best.

So, I don't go anymore after dark unless I have some of them with me and even so, not very often. We do have snakes, but I have a light. Now, I usually walk during the day.

One night, our babysitter was sleeping on the wicker lounge when the cat made a noise under him. The cat had seen a snake. He woke to find a snake underneath. The snakes love wicker. The babysitter killed the snake.

Once again, we were grateful for a good cat and besides that, it's the most beautiful cat on the mission. The cat is a long-haired gray and white cat and is so loving with the children. We also killed a beautiful but huge snake under the refrigerator. Our barefoot workmen had been working at trying to move it for fifteen minutes before they saw the snake. Fortunately, they got it before it got them!

# Rough Roads and Exciting Future Plans

Here, we are clearing the forest, making roads, planting trees and flowers and foods that will mature after we return on furlough. We may not be at this station next time, yet we can do this for those who are yet to come. I was ashamed when I thought about how we complain about these awful roads. At least there is a road. The early pioneers walked and were carried miles on end, working inland from the coast and sometimes traveled dangerous river streams. In 1878, the first missionaries settled in Congo. Now some of those early stations have block square hospitals, huge, lovely schools which take both men and women even through high school and they are looking toward a university. They are highly developed places with hundreds of outlying stations, modern printing presses, and literature in the African language.

There are hundreds of African languages and none of them were even reduced to writing before the missionaries. All the books they have though pitifully few, have been written by the missionaries except for a few in the "trade languages" put out by the State.

We have five couples in Belgium at the present who will be coming and two new couples on the field. The future looks bright. Our doctor and printer and all their equipment will soon be here and in use. Much of the equipment is even now awaiting its arrival. We'll have a hospital and a print shop. Our builder is here now. We're expecting great things in the years ahead. We're planning on going into new tribes and territories. Our schoolteacher is in Belgium too. They say he is a brain and has several degrees. He is bringing a lot of good books for the school. The girls will go to the boarding school next term, but I will keep them for a few years yet.

## Early Missionary Trials and Near Death

The pygmies are not too far from here. They are probably 400 miles as the crow flies, but 600 miles of terrible roads. We're about 300 miles as the crow flies from where Stanley met Livingston.

According to a map we saw of his explorations back in the early days, Livingston came very close to Ikozi. He certainly had an interesting and amazing life. He was almost not human in his ability and willingness to endure hardship. He even ate rats and mice and moles to survive when he was starving. We're sitting in palaces on beds of ease compared to what our predecessors endured. Even those who pioneered our mission knew little of the comforts we know today. Even during the last term on the field, most of them were without refrigerator and lights.

I don't see how we could manage without our refrigerator as food, even peas spoil within hours. When we go on forest trips, sometimes our food spoils from lunch to dinner. Meat can't be kept at all. Valuable medicines and vitamins spoil quickly if not refrigerated. In the heat, a cold drink is greatly appreciated. Also, we frequently use the ice cubes medically. We enjoy ice cream too. I've perfected a recipe that is like Dairy Queen, even with powdered milk.

So many of the early missionaries died. Others were killed. Even dear Mrs. Aimie was poisoned by hostile tribes' early days, but the cook had washed and scraped the meat because he thought it looked green. She had told him, "We haven't seen meat for weeks. Please cook it well. It's not rotten, and it doesn't stink."

She lived through it but suffered a lot. She would have died if the cook had not scraped it off and soaked it like he did. That tribe that did that was the adjoining tribe and they're fierce and still man eaters. They have not accepted the gospel, the good news of God's love for them. They still wear mud all over their bodies and long matted hair. Even the government said, "People still disappear in there sometimes."

In those early days, the missionaries' children couldn't come, and women soon died after arrival, as well as many men. But today, things are so modern in many of those same places and there are thousands of fine African Christians because of the persistence of the "never give up" missionaries and mission boards in those difficult days.

## Christmas Joy and News About the Girls

Sharon and Sandra anticipated Christmas with great excitement. Each day for a while before Christmas, we told them the Christmas story with the aid of our little manger scene. On Christmas day, Sharon told it to us in great detail.

Sandra talked a lot about baby Jesus and attempted to sing, "Away in the Manger," as she folded her little hands and laid her head on them. Each day, Sharon would ask if any more presents got off the ship. I tried to wrap up little things so they would have a lot to open.

January 4, 1955

Dear Daddy,

I sure do wish I had a good photo of you 5 by 7 or 8 by 10. Sharon asked me the other day to get out a snapshot and show her again. She said, "I've forgotten how granddaddy looks, but I remember that when I kiss him, he jumps." (Grandaddy for fun would jump in the air whenever the children kissed him on the cheek.)

Both girls are so healthy and big now. They say and do so many cute things. Sharon does exceptionally well in school. She has finished reading most of her second-grade readers on her own and has taught herself to spell on her own outside of our school course. She always makes 100 in writing tests or compositions and arithmetic too. She's a grade ahead too and that being in the second grade.

~~~

**Note from the author:** In the next chapter, I'm going to share a dark supernatural experience told to me by my mother. As I shared earlier, we have authority over the forces of evil and we don't need to be afraid. However, sometimes it's a battle to overcome them.

~~~

# Oppressive Demonic Forces

My mom and dad were followed into the valley by the elders and others, who then crossed to the other side and climbed a hill. "Please don't go! Please, mama and papa don't go. It's dangerous!" My parents had heard about an initiation ceremony and wanted to go observe it. My mother especially had a keen fascination with cultural differences. So, from her standpoint, this was an opportunity to appreciate a cross-cultural experience.

According to the spiritual teachings passed down to my parents, the supernatural had no bearing on contemporary life. So, their belief was that Africans were simply superstitious. They were unaware of the dark demonic forces present in certain ceremonies. The elders and other Africans who knew better wanted to protect them.

When I was older, my mother shared the experience with me. "As we started to go up the hill, we sensed an oppressive force so evil and strong, we could not go further. We turned around and went back to our house across the valley. Yet the dark forces were still so heavy in the house. I fell to my knees and prayed for four hours and pleaded the blood of Jesus. The dark forces finally broke, and we were free again."

My parents realized that day that Africans possess an awareness of the supernatural that's often lacking in Western culture. We think that education is everything and if we're educated, we're not affected by those forces. However, this is not true. The dark demonic forces are alive and well. They cause havoc that people are not aware of because of people's denial of their existence. Some reading this may discount this and disagree, but that's okay. Both my mother's accounts and my own personal experiences have shown me that these evil forces are real and active today.

Many Africans lived in fear of demons, seeking help from witch doctors who only further exposed them to those forces. The gospel of Jesus helped liberate many Africans from their fears.

As Christians, we possess the power and authority to conquer these forces, which is good news indeed. As the apostle Paul tells us, in Philippians 2:10,11, "At the name of Jesus every knee should bow .and that every tongue should confess that Jesus Christ is Lord, to the glory of God the Father." This is an ongoing battle, but as I shared earlier, we can be free from these dark demonic influences and take authority over them in the name of Jesus.

# The Birth of the Third Daughter

The following is a letter my mother wrote to her family in relation to the birth of Kathi, the third daughter.

~~~

I am taking advantage of this time to rest. We will go about the first of March to the mission station where the doctor is to make sure to have enough time there before the baby is born. I need to have good checkups and perhaps some liver shots, as my blood count is rather low. We're getting meat but I have had no appetite for the first months and then I've had a pretty full schedule too, with Ernest gone. I'm sure enjoying having him home for the holidays. He'll be going back soon, though, into the jungle to preach.

We'll be going to a very good, experienced American doctor with years of service in the Congo and modern hospital equipment and medicines, so it will be all right. I'll get as good care as at home in the USA. I'll have lots of help when I come home. I don't have to wash my own diapers, cook the meals, scrub the floors or anything like that because the household servants will do those things. I'll only have to look after the baby.

Ernest will stay home for several months from forest mission trips to be sure all goes well. He's very careful not to leave me here without a car and someone to drive it even now. He stays whenever the other couple has to be away.

Juanita sent me a permanent for the children, so I gave it to Sandra. It's going to be quite cute. Sharon's hair is naturally curly, so she doesn't need anything.

Mother is the librarian at the Midwest Bible and Missionary Institute now. She is also being trained as a Book Store Manager for their Christian bookstore since the present manager, a nice young man, is leaving.

Mother worked day and night at the post office 8 days during the Christmas rush and made good wages for it. She insisted on sending us every cent of it to help on the trip and paying the doctor. I hated to accept it but thought it was sweet of her. She hates it that she can't be here to care for the baby, so she insisted on having this part in it. Juanita would sure like to have a baby. There is nothing like children to make a home a happy, cheerful place to be. They really give you something to live for and look forward to as they grow and develop.

Sharon does very exceptional work in school. She makes straight 100's and is way ahead of her lessons already. She memorizes really fast and remembers things so long and so well.

## New Baby in Family

~~~

**Note from the author**: This letter is from my dad, Ernest, written to Granddaddy Roy Vickrey (my mother's dad.) To me, this is a precious treasure because, as I said previously, my dad rarely wrote letters. He was a quiet man and didn't talk much either, so it was rare to know what was on his mind.

His gifts were more in the scholarly teaching area, which benefited him well in translating the Bible into the local language. He was detail oriented, which helped him in translation, and you can see this in his account. Here is his letter.

~~~

April 15, 1955

We have another sweet little girl in our family. Her name is Kathleen Juanita. Juanita is after Virginia's sister. She weighed 8lbs. Those are the headlines. Here are the details. Virginia woke up at 4:30 a.m. and felt a little uncomfortable, and her first pains started at 5:00. I woke up at six and she told me. Then I went to the hospital to tell Dr. Hughlette. He came and examined her and listened to the pulse beat of the baby. He said it was probably a girl. That prepared us, so we were not surprised when it was another girl.

We had read our Bibles and prayed together before the doctor arrived. Sandra woke up soon, and she was sure happy when she heard the baby would be born today. Later, Sharon woke up when the nurse came and could hardly believe that the baby would be born that day, but needless to say, she was overjoyed to hear the news.

~~~

**Note from the author:** In the letter, he shares that the baby was born, and he got to see her being born.

~~~

My dad continues.

Our household servant took Sharon and Sandra out walking, so I ran out and found them to tell them it was a girl. They were so happy and could hardly wait until they got Virginia cleaned up so that they could come in and see the baby. They sure do like their baby sister. Sandi said today, "Now I've got a grown-up sister and a baby sister. Sure, wish I had a chance to get a brudder."

I was just telling Virginia today that little boys could never be as pretty as little baby girls.; Of course, being her parents, we are prejudice, but the first thing the doctor's wife said was, "She sure is a pretty baby."

~~~

**Note from the author:** My dad had wanted a boy with each of us, so this statement from him is confirmation of his acceptance and pleasure in his daughters.

~~~

Two hours after the baby was born, we were on our way to Lubefu, the state post seventeen miles away, to send a telegram and register the baby. It's a good thing that we sent a telegram so you all could hear right away, as there are two bridges out between here and Lusambo. Thus, we did not get any mail last Saturday and now here it is today and no mail again this week.

Virginia is nursing the baby, and the milk is coming in today. She is recovering faster this time because she had an easier delivery. We will probably go back to Kamulila 12-14 days after Kathi's birth. We are rejoicing that all is well and with the little girl that the Lord gave us.

# After Kathi's Birth -
# New Congo Hospital

April 17, 1955,

After Kathi's birth, Virginia's letter to her father.

Dear Daddy,

We surely enjoy our little girl. She is a very pretty, healthy and good baby. We had planned on a boy, but I guess boys are scarce in my family. Babies are surely sweet. We have so much fun with her.

We will take a week or so to go home in order to break the trip and rest along the way for my sake and the baby's. It's a 4-day trip on bumpy, dusty roads with many potholes. It takes us 8 hrs to go 125 miles.

Kathi didn't do anything negative the whole time. She has such an angelic disposition. She's the easiest one I've ever had.

Mom with baby Kathi, Sandi and Sharon with African
mud huts in the background.

Of course, when they get together, they all bring out the worst in each other as kids are prone to do, but individually they behave real well. We sure do enjoy our new baby.

Kathi, as the baby, gets attention and Sharon is always in the limelight. So, Sandra, as the middle child, suffers pangs of jealousy and frustration sometimes. We're trying to watch it and go out of the way to show her extra attention.

## New Congo Hospital

Our doctor arrived on the field in May. It was one of the greatest events in the history of the mission. Until now, there were about 800 miles between missionary doctors in our region. We were perplexed about where we should build the hospital. The Lord miraculously caused a government post to be abandoned just at that time in the exact center of our territory. There are many brick buildings already erected, hospital wards, a dispensary, missionary dwellings and their buildings ready for immediate possession. The state used prison labor to build those, and they are willing to sell them to us for about one-fourth of what it would cost us to build them. The cost of $8000 must be paid at once. $3000 is on hand at the moment.

## Going to the USA

Summer, 1956, Prayer Letter

We arrived in New York by air, July 9th. It was joy unspeakable to plant our feet on American soil and to be reunited with friends and loved ones here!

After much prayer, we felt the Lord would have us settle in Wichita, Kansas, our hometown for now because we have many friends and contacts in this area. Also, my mother had a house for us. She prayed, and the renters moved and that enabled us to move in.

Our children are happily settled in school. They are in the 4th and 2nd grades. Sharon said her first day at school was the happiest day of her life.

Three African evangelistic teams went into the forest and the mining territory around Kamulila this summer just before we left. They reported enthusiastic responses and about 70 Africans professed faith in Christ during those meetings!

~~~

**Note from the author:** There is quite a gap here when my parents were in the USA visiting churches to raise support and changing missions. The reason my parents decided to change mission is that they felt they needed to listen to the Holy Spirit's leading for them in their work.

The mission they were with in the first term believed the mission board was the ones who knew God's will for each missionary in their mission.

So, my parents decided to join a mission who believed as my parents did that the individual missionary needed to hear the voice of God and His will for them. So, they changed to go under the "Africa Inland Mission" for the second term. (Back then, the missionaries went for a longer period of time, typically five years because of the limited transportation by boat and the expense. Changing missions was a lengthy process, so I don't have another letter until 3 years after the last prayer letter. She wrote the following letter after a health examination.

~~~

## May 1959 Health Issues

1959 Virginia's personal letter to her daddy.

It looks like we won't get to go back to Africa. We sure felt bad about it, but this bigger mission doesn't think my health record sounds very good. I guess they don't want to risk it. It's a miracle that we ever got to go at all because of that. I'm okay now but they are afraid of recurrence under pressure, I guess.

~~~

**Note from the author:** Obviously, her health issues did not stand in the way of their return to Africa, as you will read letters from her starting in 1960. To me, this shows that despite her health struggles, she was still willing and able to serve the Lord and the African people. Our health challenges do not limit God. This can be such an encouragement to those who think their health can hold them back from serving God. Don't hold back. If you need to limit yourself, you can still serve God and others. My mother is an example of this. Because of her determination to continue serving, she made a significant positive impact on so many people.

~~~

# Congo's Independence June 1960

We have gone on our first evangelistic trip to Zandeland. What an encouragement it was to have five women stay after the service to accept the Lord Jesus Christ as their Savior. Ernest also had the privilege of taking a tour of 28 of the out schools in surrounding areas of Dungu station with the other missionary, Norman Weiss. They held six to seven meetings a day and traveled 300 miles in all.

A Dutchman from Dungu was badly beaten by soldiers in the nearby town and put into jail. When he returned here, we befriended him because he had nothing. He loved to read the Child's Story Bible that we read to Kathi and wants to buy one. He said that by reading it, he realized for the first time that Jesus Christ was truly God's Son. We had the opportunity to talk to him about spiritual things.

I am busy translating Bible lessons for the African teachers of the girls. I am also printing Zande titles of the Bible stories to distribute to the outlying village evangelists. I take African women out each week for Bible teaching in the surrounding villages.

# Evacuation Drills June 1960

Sharon and Sandra are having evacuation drills at Rethy, like students at home have fire drills. They keep a change of clothes packed in a plastic bag and are each assigned to a car and a guardian. Things are quiet there now, but that station had been evacuated before when there was trouble in Burnia. The children seem happy at the school this term. There are half as many as last year. Much to Sharon's chagrin, she's the only girl in the 7th and 8th grade, but she has several girlfriends in other grades.

Everything is quiet in our area at the present time. We are thankful that all of our Africa Inland Mission stations are occupied. We are especially thankful for this in view of the fact that some missions in Congo have evacuated all their missionaries and others have evacuated half or more of their personnel.

~~~

**Note from the author:** Later we did have to evacuate from Rethy, as I shared in the first chapter of this book. The next letter from my mother is after their return to the Congo after the evacuation.

~~~

# Word of God Strengthens
## December 1960

L ife has returned to normal in many ways after the evacuation. Keep praying for the many turbulent problems. We do praise the Lord that many missionaries who were evacuated from some troubled areas are returning to their stations. There are 45 Presbyterian missionaries, including 20 women, who have returned to their work in the troubled Kasai province.

The Christian and Missionary Alliance missionaries are located between turbulent Leopoldville and Matadi. Yet they never evacuated their stations. God seemed to build a wall of protection around them in the only area where missionaries were actually molested. Other missionaries still carry on in troubled Leopoldville. The Conservative Baptist missionaries are all still at their stations, as are all A.I.M. (Africa Inland Mission) missionaries.

We do praise because we have peace in our hearts, no matter how troubled the circumstances in our life. We like Phillip's translation of 2 Corinthians 4:15-17. "We wish you could see how all this is working out for your benefit and how the more grace God gives, the more thanksgiving will redound to His glory. This is the reason why we never collapse. The outward man does indeed suffer wear and tear, but every day the inward man receives fresh strength. These little troubles which are really transitory are winning for us a permanent and glorious reward out of all proportion to our pain."

Truly, every day, our hearts are strengthened as we drink in the Word of God and pour out our souls to Him in prayer.

~~~

This above letter and the following letter were in a December 1960 prayer letter to supporting churches.

~~~

## Christmas Celebrations

December is a happy month! Christmas carols ring out during the morning in Pazande (the local tribal language) as our enthusiastic schoolboys and girls practice for the Christmas program accompanied by Ernest on his trumpet. Sharon and Sandra have returned home for the holiday month (from boarding school) and are cozily situated in the attractive little guest house built right by our bedroom. We are anticipating a very happy Christmas season.

Long before dawn, happy schoolboys and girls will sing carols for us to bring Christmas cheer. Then we will sit out under the mango trees to enjoy the Christmas program in Technicolor as the boys and girls sing the joyous carols and the shepherds and wise men clad in our house coats and head scarfs tell once again the old but ever new glad tidings of our Savior's birth to the thousands or so gathered there.

We are in need of a new African caretaker for our girls' dormitory. Pray with us for a dedicated Christian woman with a real love for the Lord and the girls will be found.

May the God of Hope fill you with all joy and peace in believing during the coming year.

# Christmas and Mission Work
## December 6, 1960

Dear Daddy,

Greetings from hot Zandeland. I wish I could package up our dry season heat and exchange it for a little bit of snow!

Christmas season has rolled around, and I have no way to get a token of my love to you. I bought a nice carving for you, packaged it up and when I went to mail it, they said they would not accept any packages sent out of Congo.

Letter to Mom's dad from Kenya.

Too many people are sending their belongings home, and the Africans want to keep the white man's possessions here even if he leaves.

Last year, I sent a check to Aunt Gaynel and Uncle George to use to get you a gift, but I didn't hear from them or you about it and the check was never cashed. So, this year I have sent a check to Gladys Meals, a friend of ours in Wichita who is always willing to do things for us.

It wasn't much because we've had so many expenses with the car, 4 new tires, new battery, whole exhaust system and other work done on it. These roads tear the car up. We still have monthly payments, too. But we want you to know we are thinking about you and love you.

Our girls are home for the holidays from December 1 to January 8. We have been invited to go the Banda for New Years with Dr. and Mrs. Brown and daughters. Then we go to Rethy for a field conference on the 8th-15th. After that we'll probably be alone on the station as the other missionaries, the Weises, will be moving to Napopo for the Bible school.

We will have the leper work for a few months. The African nurses do most of it, though they are so needy, it will be a privilege to help. Our doctor works with it and even handles the sores and never catches it. It is usually caught by children over prolonged close contact. Then it crops out 30 years later.

We have fixed up a darling room for our girls in the guest house by our bedroom at the side of the house. Our house is so cute and nicely furnished.

The Reader's Digest is coming as of November. We sure enjoy it! Thanks so much! Love, Virginia

~~~

**Note from the author:** The following chapter contains a letter written to the churches in January 1961 relating to changing mission stations when my parents were reassigned to a different station.

~~~

# Changing Mission Stations

Our mission assigned us to Niangara, a station that needs much work and prayer. This will be one of the greatest and most difficult

Sandi, Dad, Sharon, Mom and Kathi
in front of the house at Niangara.

challenges of our life. This means we have to learn another language as well. We will be able to minister to most of the people in Pazande which we are now studying.

Since there are many tribes at the large state post, we need to learn Bangala, which is a trade language and used inter-tribally. It is far easier than the tribal language we had to learn this year and has many words from the other African languages that we have been learning. However, if one is to speak any language properly, there is a lot of work involved in learning it.

Dad in our living room at
Niangara..

Please pray for us in this new challenge.

The Mangbetu tribe near there has no scripture at all in their language. Most of the language has not even been reduced to writing. There are very few in the tribe who have responded to the gospel, and they show little interest.

The single lady who will be our only co-worker at Niangara has been assigned to learn their language and to translate the Word of God into their language. Miss Grace Congleton has been here for 20 years and knows both Pazande and Bangala. But she has not been able to find anybody willing and able to teach her Mangbetu. Will you pray with us for this tribe and for

Sandi, Sharon and Kathi
on the porch at Niangara.

Miss Congleton in her efforts to learn their language?

There are no elders on the station, and the present pastor came from a tribe south of here to replace the regular pastor while he was in Bible school. The station needs good, trained leadership badly. Will you pray with us as we work with the present pastor that the Lord will use us to train other leaders? We cannot converse with the pastor except through an interpreter until we learn Bangala. There are 22 out village preacher teachers who need much guidance and training.

The station school has only about 40 students with no trained teachers. There is much work that needs to be done to make the school more effective. So far, most of the children attend the large Catholic school in town. Very few women at Niangara know how to read, so we will probably have to start a women's school. Virginia wants to train the women to go out two by two and teach the word of God as they do at Dungu.

The field council felt that Dungu has enough trained leaders to carry on the work alone now. The Dungu Christians are very sad that we are being transferred, and they find it hard to accept. Pray for them during this difficult time of adjustment. Our home at Niangara is located right in the state post in which thousands of Africans live. The house is a large brick house with

Mom with the beautiful scenery and river at Niangara.

an aluminum roof, but it's very old. It is full of termites which at times have eaten the curtains off the walls and the bedding off the bed. We hope to be able to cement the walls and finish the floors better to curb their activities. One good thing is that we will have the most beautiful scenery from our large front porch with a river lined with palms. It is equal to any travel folder. The palm nuts are delicious when they are roasted. Also, the mango trees give us an abundance of sumptuous mangoes that the children pick them up off the ground to eat them. We have so many that I make mango jam, mango butter, mango sauce and I use them in recipes.

Thank you for your Christmas cards and letters! We had a very nice Christmas. At the present time, incoming mail is being censored and delayed, but please keep writing.

~~~

**Note from the author:** The following letter is written during a trip to Nairobi to get the children. The mission school went on for three months and then they let the children go home for a month.

~~~

# Nairobi Refuge January, 1961

Sharon has grown out of everything I had for her. There are three sewing circles in Wayne, Michigan, sewing for her, but it will be three months before they get here as they haven't even mailed them, so I'm buying patterns and materials. I borrowed a nice electric sewing machine to sew for her. Ready-made clothes are too expensive here.

I could buy them ready-made from the Montgomery Wards catalog for the price of what I pay for zippers, thread, patterns and material. But I'm enjoying sewing and she needs them now. It's a good way to spend my vacation.

We were able to get top-notch medical and dental care here in Nairobi. Ernie had trouble with an abscessed tooth for a long time, so we were glad to get it out. He was miserable at first, but now he is healing. He lost 20 lbs, so we want to have him checked to make sure that his dysentery didn't occur. I lost 10 lbs when I was sick with the flu or malaria. Now, I've gained back 5 lbs, I wish I wouldn't, but we have Dairy Queen here, other treats, and delicious food.

We are staying at the Africa Inland Mission guest house in Nairobi. We'll be able to swim here. Also, there is a world-famous wild animal park that is an international tourist attraction. The lions roam around, and the monkeys fly to the car window for bananas. We've had elephants right by the road through Uganda park and sometimes on the road. One time we had to stop for the elephants to cross the road. Of course, we were at a distance, but it was fascinating to watch as the elephant herd lumbered across, and a line of cars waited.

~~~

**Note from the author:** The next letter is to her mom and sister after they went back to their mission station. The letter shows that sometimes all is not smooth at the mission station.

~~~

# A Great Trial and Victory
## May 1961

We had a great trial during the last week and the Lord wonderfully helped us work it out in the end. To give you a little background, our mission requires that people learn how to read their bibles and purchase a New Testament before baptism during their long period of instruction.

China Inland Mission did that in China too as converts are more likely to stay strong in the faith. However, the former missionary, Al, let that slide. So here we have a church full of people who can't read. We even have this one elder who is such a poor testimony. He has no schooling at all and reads terribly and doesn't even understand.

Ernie took a firm stand by the rules of the mission and refused any who were young enough to learn until they did so. We did make exceptions for the old and we have lots of old ones coming for baptism.

Then Grace saw some of the younger ones working in the church food storehouse where they keep food used to feed people who come into the conferences.

She asked what they were doing, and they said they were "working for our baptism." That's what the Catholics require. They get lots of free labor out of them and make them work for their baptism. That appeals to their way of thinking, so our African leaders were doing the same. They claim Al let them get by with it. There have been some who have closed their eyes to it, thinking it's just the African way and you can't change them.

Ernie had told them that all the church members, including the leaders, should work on church projects, not just baptism candidates. They aren't even church members yet. As usual, they agreed to his face and did as they pleased behind his back. He went down and said he just would not baptize any of them under these conditions. They had no one else licensed by the church to do it, so the pastor just blew up. He yelled and fussed at Ernie and talked about everything and then called a meeting and yelled at a bunch of people in the church about it.

Fortunately, Grace was on our side. They dashed a runner to Napopo to ask someone else to come baptize and to make a case against us to the other missionary. We didn't know that but felt this should go to the African district church council and be straightened out, feeling that they would stand with us. The other men on the stations are strong leaders and spiritual men. We wrote to Norman.

When he first got their letter, he wrote back sort of feeling that we should baptize them, but when he got our side of the story, he said we were right for two reasons. The people believed they were earning their baptism and second the work was not voluntary but forced. Ernie said he could not conscientiously baptize them under those conditions and someone else would have to come and do it if they did not agree.

Well, Grace was glad we took a stand. After a few tense days of strained relations and long arguing with all the elders and Grace and Ernie at the house, finally the best elder of all said to Ernie, "You really think this is wrong in the eyes of God?"

"Yes, I do."

"Well, if we sin, God forgives us. Can't you forgive us and baptize?"

There were 69 candidates after weeding out the young ones who had not learned to read. We were having a big conference, and they were in a spot to save face. Ernie said, "Yes, I will with these conditions. You call the whole church to do this work on the church that needs to be done tomorrow. Then you have a meeting and let me talk to the candidates about the meaning of baptism. I will explain that baptism does not save, and it is like salvation. It is a free gift. Then you never assign work as a condition of baptism again."

What they will do in the future is another question, but all of his conditions were fulfilled.

The meeting started at 8:50 AM and lasted until 3:20 PM, with only a brief break to walk to the river and baptize. The first service lasted 2 hours and the preacher who had only had a second-grade education rattled on for an hour and 15 minutes in a language we did not yet know.

Then they had baptism, communion, a church meeting, and the election of elders. We left after communion as the rest did not concern us and the Browns were here from Bandi for the day. I fed them and reveled in their fellowship. I was so lonely since I don't have fellowship with others here. I had prayed they would stop by on their medical tour of Zandi land. We don't have a dispensary, so they don't always stop.

At that meeting the church voted Daniel, who had been big pain, off the station by a vote of 81 to 8. They don't like him because he pushes himself forward and orders everyone around so much. He is the one who often hadn't appointed anyone to preach on Sunday or another day. When he preached, he did so in filthy, ragged undershirts. He led singing way off pitch and skipped two lines often while reading and never knew the difference.

We had a very spiritually minded troublemaker teacher whose wife held a boy's hands in boiling water for a minute because she was mad at the child. She has never repented, and she was making trouble. She is a troublemaker wherever she goes. He had also caused problems, but Ernie was not able to persuade the elders and pastor to let him go.

The only influence we have in this situation is prayer, and so we pray.

~~~

**Note from the author:** This statement from my mother is a good example of what we need to do when confronted with situations out of our control. When faced with difficult situations we cannot change, we need to turn to prayer and wait for God to move. The Word of God reassures that prayer is effective. The Amplified version of the Bible gives us powerful insight into James 5:16b. "The heartfelt *and* persistent prayer of a righteous man (believer) can accomplish much [when put into action and made effective by God—it is dynamic and can have tremendous power]."

~~~

# Congo Crisis and Beloved Doctor Dies May 1964

We are thoroughly enjoying our new work! This is a large responsive work with over 100 out- village preachers. There are more than 700 children in the station's elementary schools.

We are 300 miles closer to our children and only 50 miles from Uganda where we can buy groceries and have really good mail service.

## The Congo Crisis continues!

The Republic of Congo is once again in the midst of political turmoil. Communist backed youth groups (Jeunesse) have killed many government officials, Catholic missionaries and at least one Protestant missionary. MAF (Missionary Aviation Fellowship) evacuated others, including friends of ours, in the nick of time. There were demonstrations at Rethy, the children's school, and some of the Africans on the mission station were beaten. Their school opened one week late because of this.

Pray for the government to have wisdom and the ability to control and overcome the movement. The UN troops leave Congo in June! Only prayer can keep missions operating throughout the Congo. It will be bad for all of Africa if the communists succeed in taking over Congo. This area is much more hostile than our former one.

The Sudan situation is still serious. All the missionaries were expelled from Sudan. Pray that the American embassy will succeed in getting their equipment out. Constant warfare is in progress as southern Sudan seeks to free themselves from Muslim rulers. Villages have been burned, and atrocities abound. Congolese missionaries Simona and Phoebe and family were allowed to remain but need our prayers very much.

Our field director, Rev. Peter Brashler, sought to strengthen our missionaries by reading over the "ham," radio Jeremiah 39:17, 18. "But I will deliver thee in that day, saith the Lord: For I will surely deliver thee, and thou shalt not fall by the sword, but thy life shall be for a prize unto thee because thou hast put thy trust in me, saith the Lord."

He also reported that he had received word from the U.S. Embassy in Kampala that they felt missionaries were in no danger as long as the local population wanted them to stay. We also understand that the rebel leaders issued a statement that they "want the protestant missionaries to stay and carry on with schools, hospitals, and preaching." However, we do need to remember that our own country is becoming involved in giving assistance to the Central Government and this could jeopardize the standing of our missionaries with any rebel government.

## A devoted doctor dies!

Dr. Kleinschmidt, a beloved doctor died. He was mourned by all. All the stores in Aba township closed, as well as all Catholic schools. The nuns and priests attended the funeral, along with over 70 Europeans from far and near. Soldiers and state officials paid him tribute. For 40 years, he manifested the spirit of Christ here in selfless service and care for others. We now have over 700 miles with no mission doctor, two hospitals and about 10 mission dispensaries and leprosarium, with no doctor to visit every month or two for surgery and difficult cases.

Missionaries are missing everywhere! Several stations will be without missionaries this year. An advanced girl's school has been closed. A desperately needed secondary school cannot open unless health and financial obstacles are removed from missionaries hoping to come. We need to advance while the door is still open, but we have to retreat. Pray for the Lord of the harvest to bring out laborers, especially doctors, nurses, and teachers!

# Niangara and Outreach at Adi, Prayer Letter

Niangara is still without a missionary. There are 65,000 people in that area, about 20 outlying-village preachers, and about four bush schools enrolling about 125 children. We had 85 children in school on the station in a densely populated town area. There is no ordained pastor. There were about 300 baptized Christians, 90% were illiterate. There were 45 Belgian Catholic missionaries in town and just the two of us, Protestant missionaries, and now none!

The people there need more support as they are very immoral and there was constant backsliding into immoral practices. The people here at our present mission station are more steadfast. They seem more intelligent and advanced.

One African man and his wife have gone from here as a missionary to Niangara. Mikaya and Durusila are reaching an almost totally unreached tribe in a very hard place. They are in a town where we should have a mission station. They have stood through constant trials and testing in a very hard place. They need our prayers! Ernest just returned from a conference at Niangara to encourage the Christians. Please pray for the local church situation there as it has deteriorated terribly.

## The Contrast of Adi with Niangara

What is our new station like? Contrast Adi with Niangara for a minute. 28,000 in our territory, 110 outlying-village chapels, and each one has a school to teach people how to read their Bibles. There are 7 central bush schools that go through the 5th grade. There are 167 out-village preachers and teachers. We have 700 pastors working in this area. Reception to the gospel has been thrilling here in times past. Present-day pressures have corrupted many of the younger generation. They lack the interest, strength, and the zeal of the old-timers.

In the medical department, we have 610 lepers registered with about 400 coming regularly. The dispensary also treated hundreds of sick people from many different tribes and from nearby Sudan and Uganda.

Maternity emergencies cause many night trips into the bush. Our nurse finds the medical work exceedingly frustrating as we have no doctor to visit and examine the serious cases. Medicines are hard to get. We are having a smallpox epidemic with several deaths already. We have only been able to get a few vaccines, so the epidemic is a problem to keep under control.

# Rebel Movements
## Closer to Us - August 1964.

U nless something stops them, our days in Congo are numbered. Our new government gives hope of being able to restore some stability, and economic improvement, if only they could stop the rebel advances! Pray for wisdom and ability for them.

According to Time magazine, the rebels now control 1/3 of Congo. These movements are still very anti-mission as well as anti-government. Stanleyville, our capital, has fallen as I write this. Our location is northeast of Stanleyville, near the Uganda border. Since mail is more reliable in Uganda, we get our mail over there.

We were astounded to learn of the fall of Stanleyville and the threat of advancement. From all we have learned during our recent visit to our fields in Central Africa, the activities of the guerrilla warriors have been organized and launched by the Chinese communists in Ruanda. Once again, the Africa Inland Mission and numerous other mission societies find themselves in the midst of another Congo crisis in our field by "ham" radio. There has been no rebel activity in the A.I.M. (Africa Inland Mission), but everyone is sitting tight. The present government officials have issued special passes to all of our missionaries to cross into Uganda if it is necessary.

Bible school graduation was at the end of July. This station has sent several African missionaries to other tribes and to Sudan. The Congolese missionaries were permitted to stay in Sudan. Some have undergone persecution. They also restricted their children from going to school. However, the missionaries continued to strengthen the young Sudanese churches.

~~~

**Note from the author:** Above is the only letter where my mother shared about the rebel movements. I'll share in the next chapter some of my recollections of the final evacuation and after it.

~~~

# After the Final Evacuation
# Losing Everything 1965

We had lots of turmoil and life threatening situations during the final evacuation. We had been held at gunpoint over and over since Congo got its independence. We had many frightening circumstances, but in the end, our lives were in even more danger. I don't have letters sharing about the evacuation and what we went through, so I rely on my memory and the reports of other missionaries through their books and a few online articles. I was sixteen when we evacuated for the final time to Nairobi, Kenya. After a year when my parents were in Nairobi, I still attended the Rift Valley Academy. I was seventeen when we came to the U.S.A.

My parents left their mission station in the Congo for the final time when order came from the government to "kill every white man on sight." My parents could only take what fit in the back of their truck. They left most of their earthly possessions behind. One poignant note is that our pet dog, Kim, a German shepherd, ran after the truck as we drove down the road. We were not able to take him.

My parents went to live in Nairobi, Kenya, for a year, hoping to be able to get back into Congo. Many of the British who had homes there would go home for three months at a time. They were eager to find someone to stay in their homes. Stealing was so common and serious in Nairobi.

For example, I had a new roommate whose parents had come to Kenya as missionaries. After they went in to eat at a restaurant, they came out and all their luggage with their clothes was stolen. All the teenage girl's clothes were gone. Even though they had locked the car, the thieves got in and took everything. That is how bad the theft was there.

So, every three months, my parents moved to a different house to house sit. Since they had lost everything, they didn't have much to move. It was an ideal provision from God because the homes were beautiful. The homeowners were delighted to have someone house sit for them.

During that year in Nairobi, we had another big blessing! My baby sister, Dianne Ruth, was born, giving our family a total of four girls. My dad wanted to keep trying so he could get a boy, but he was not disappointed. As he said before, "I guess little girls are pretty sweet after all."

She was a beautiful baby, and I had the privilege of holding her in the car on the way home. Also, I had the delightful pleasure of sharing the joy with my classmates at Rift Valley Academy. My mother had the best doctor. Dr. Barnett was a missionary on the Kijabe mission station where RVA was located.

Dr. Barnett delivered Dianne at Nairobi, Kenya

We also had the joy of being able to be with my Aunt Juanita and Uncle Jim and their children, Ken, Barbara and Linda. Later, they had another son, David. They were missionaries with Missionary Aviation Fellowship and were stationed in Nairobi.

My parents waited for a year in Nairobi, hoping to be able to go back to their house at the Adi mission station in Congo. However, after a year, the doors were still closed tight to Congo as the Simbas ruled and it was very dangerous to return. Not only that, but we also learned that rebels had taken all of our things.

The Simbas were an exceptionally dangerous organization of young men under the influence of drugs who terrorized everyone including their own people.

Mom wrote in one of her letters that it would be one thing if they could use the things. But they took many things they wouldn't be able to use. For example, they took the refrigerator when they wouldn't have electricity to run it. They took all their books from their library when they couldn't read English. She lamented that it took over twenty years to accumulate their theology books. My dad used those books to do his Bible studies and to teach the Africans. Some of the things they simply destroyed.

We had nothing to go back to except ruins. We were close to our furlough time, so my parents decided to go back to the U.S.A. Any time you lose all your possessions, your home and your ministry, there is a sense of loss. One of the things that bothered her the most was a question that burned in her mind: *Were our efforts in vain?*

# Pebbles in a Pond

"Your lives were like pebbles in the pond. We are still feeling the ripples." Tears ran down my mother's cheeks as she read this letter from the elders in the Congolese church where they had served. This letter came several months after my parents evacuated for the final time to the United States in 1965.

She grieved over the loss of everything, including the ministry. In the midst of it, God brought her strong comfort. She had been wondering if it was worth it after all the destruction they experienced. The analogy from the elders assured her that their labor was not in vain.

Later, I shared this story about the pebbles in a pond with a writer at a large greeting card company. He wrote a poem about your life being like a pebble in a pond having a ripple effect. That creative analogy came from this unknown African elder. His insight has blessed many people around the world. This often happens with tragedy. Though situations are not good and even evil, God can bring good out of it to bless many.

Whenever you experience loss and trauma, there is a natural grieving process. There is a lot of questioning along with it. Grieving is a process that we didn't

176 | SHARON ROSE GIBSON

understand back then, and we didn't know how to grieve well.

We also didn't know how to deal with trauma such as the trauma of being held at gunpoint over and over, the trauma of having our lives threatened on a regular basis, and the trauma of hearing horrific stories of abuse of other missionaries, the Africans, and other people.

Why were we spared when others weren't? Yes, God spoke directly to my parents and assured them of protection. By faith, they believed Him. For those who didn't survive, I have questions.

Some people, when they have questions or don't understand, they turn from God. I believe when you don't understand, you should run to God. I have what I call an "I don't understand" box. Anything I don't understand, I figuratively put in that box. When I get to heaven, I will pull those questions out of the box and ask Him.

I realize that He sees the big picture and we don't. Therefore, I need to be childlike and trust Him with what I don't understand. I cling to His character and the fact that He is good and faithful. When things are confusing, trusting in His character gives me stability.

As an adult and I look back on the aftermath of these experiences, I can see the way God was indeed faithful and good to us. A friend sent us money for each of us to buy clothes and others helped as well, since we had to buy furniture, kitchen items, and many other things. God also opened doors of work opportunities for each of my parents.

In the next chapter, I share insights about overcoming fears and a miracle about my grandfather. Then I will share a tribute I wrote for my mother on Mother's Day. Additionally, I'll share a tribute for my dad I wrote on Father's Day.

# Overcoming Fears from Trauma

I want to share these two incidents to warn parents about situations that may cause fear in their little ones. I have a vivid memory of being in my father's arms at about age five. Surrounding us were men with huge, ugly masks. They danced around in some kind of ceremony. I don't know what it was, but I imagine it was something like Halloween here in the U.S.A. The men in the huge ugly masks frightened me, and I shrank from them. My father said, "It's silly to be afraid." I didn't feel reassured or protected in that situation.

My father didn't purposefully try to scare me, but sometimes parents and adults think it's fun to scare little kids. I've heard of other parents who either forced or allowed children to watch horror movies. This can cause kids to be anxious and fearful. I do want to clarify that some children are more sensitive than others. I happen to be one of them. Still, I'd like to encourage parents to be careful with their children when exposing them to things that could frighten them.

Another time I was about fourteen. The villagers had a funeral for a man who died in the village. My mother wanted to go down and observe it. I didn't want to, but she took me with her. I saw the man lying on the ground. His mouth was tied up, but stuff still came out of his mouth. This frightened and revolted me. The Congolese women had a practice of throwing themselves on the ground and wailing for three days when someone died. So, the shrieks and the sights of the women added to the trauma of the scene.

Cultural differences fascinated my mother, which was a good thing but, in this situation, it was not a good thing for me. Children often need to be shielded from what may be too much for them to handle. My mom would never intentionally hurt me, but I had nightmares after this and developed a death phobia. To this day, whenever I go to funerals, I will not look at the body. I will sit in the back and sneak out before they have people file past the casket.

From then on in Congo, I would hear the drums beat at night, and they made me feel uncomfortable. Sometimes they beat the drums because of a funeral. Other times, they beat the drums to call the spirits.

We didn't have electricity, but we did have kerosene lanterns. I always wanted to keep a lantern in my room at night until I went to sleep. I can remember my dad saying, "This is ridiculous! There's nothing to be afraid of!" But he didn't understand that I felt genuinely afraid. Fortunately, my mother was more understanding, so she allowed me to have the light I needed.

The reason I share these incidents is that I want people to be aware that the way to help children overcome fears is not to discount them. Rather, they need to be comforted and assured.

My father didn't know any better and probably had been treated like that when he was a child, when he was afraid. If my father had lovingly held me and assured me, it would have made a difference. The Bible says, "Perfect love casts out fear" (I John 4:18 NKJV paraphrase). Again, he would never intentionally hurt me, and what he did was a lack of knowledge of what I needed. Like all of us, my parents were perfectly imperfect, but they gave me what I needed the most. They gave me a stable, loving home.

One time, a friend shared an effective strategy for overcoming fear. She told me, "I put on worship music and read God's Word, especially the Psalms, and eventually the fear goes away." When you feel connected to the love of God for you and reassured, you feel secure and safe. God reassures us throughout the Bible not to be afraid because He is with us. When He says, "Don't be afraid," it is based on the assurance that He is with us.

Unfortunately, I didn't know this with a young girl in my care. I remember flying with her when she was about six. She was frightened and crying. I said the same thing and told her she didn't need to be afraid. This did not help the situation, but since I had been treated that way, I continued the pattern.

Rebuking a child's fear is not the way to give them the strength to overcome it. The word *comfort* in Latin means to strengthen. In most situations, rebuking only makes a child or adult more fearful. They fear they are doing something wrong because they have a feeling of fear. They then tend to stuff their feelings rather than deal with them.

Later in life, I learned the importance of acknowledging a person's feelings and offering reassurance. One time when my six-year-old grandson visited me, I walked with him in the dark. "Grandma, I'm afraid of the dark."

"I understand. The dark can be scary sometimes." I acknowledged his fear. I held his hand and continued, "You know, once there was a boy named David. He wrote in the Psalms, 'When I am afraid, I will trust in You.' You can trust in God because He loves you and will help you."

Later, another day, he came over to my house again and we walked outside in the dark. I had forgotten about the previous conversation. He said, "Grandma,

I'm not afraid of the dark anymore because God is with me."

The approach of reassuring him had given him the strength and confidence to overcome his fears.

# Grandfather's Miracle

I will give you a little background about my grandfather's miracle. My grandfather had been a strong supporter of his daughters in their mission work. He supported both my mom, Virginia with Africa Inland Mission, and my Aunt Juanita. My Uncle Jim and Aunt Juanita worked for Missionary Aviation Fellowship in Kenya. However, Grandaddy didn't make a profession of faith. Here is a story I wrote when he was in his later years, right before his death.

One Saturday, I felt a strong urgency to drive down to Wichita, Kansas, about a two-hour drive from where I was in Topeka on business. I resisted the urge because I had so much to do. Since it was the weekend, I would have time to catch up on some projects.

My aunt, my grandfather's only living adult child, had to move out of state. She had asked me to be the power of attorney for my grandfather when he needed to go into a nursing home. My mother had died, and I was the only relative living close. Normally, I would visit him sometimes on weekends and take him shopping for things he needed.

However, Grandaddy had been in a coma recently, so he did not need me to take him shopping. Still, I felt this strong sense that I should go see him. I finally yielded to the urge and drove down to see him.

When I arrived at the nursing home and went into his room, he lay back on the bed with his eyes closed. I sat on the edge of the bed and held his hand. I wondered if he was close to death. I risked an important question. "Grandaddy, do you know Jesus?" He sat straight up in bed. For one moment, all the mental fog cleared. His eyes opened, he smiled and declared emphatically, "YES!"

He fell back on his pillow and went into a coma once again. I sat there for a while pondering these reassuring words. My aunt prayed for his salvation her whole life, and while she was alive, my mom had too.

I drove back up to Topeka that night. The next day, the nursing home called me to tell me that my grandfather had slipped away, dying quietly in his sleep. When my aunt came for the funeral, I was able to tell her the good news. She told me that she used to sit by his bed reading the Bible to him and praying for him. Now, she could rest in peace knowing that she would indeed see her father again in heaven.

I also felt assured that he and my mother are enjoying each other in heaven. I can look forward to seeing both of them as well as my aunt, my father and grandmother.

Every time I reflect on this, I'm reminded of the importance of obeying those God-driven urges. Behind every step of obedience is a blessing.

# Tribute to Mom
## Compassionate Service

Educating women was a revolutionary concept in a culture that did not value a woman's worth. One of my earliest memories is in a church made out of mud walls, open on the sides with a straw roof. My mom taught the women to

Mom teaching the African women with their children.

read as they sat together on the wooden benches. When I was seven or eight, she let me come alongside her. I can still see the scene in my eyes as I went to individual women to help them learn to read. Sometimes she taught them in the open from the Bible. I would like to invite you to think about this.

What if you wanted to learn more about God but you didn't know how to read? Can you imagine what that would be like to long to know more about God? Can you imagine if you had longed to receive the encouragement and comfort of scripture, and you were not able to read it? The only way you could get the Word of God is by going to church.

This is the way it was in the jungles of Africa where I grew up. For some, going to church meant walking for an hour or two on Sunday. They would get up at the break of dawn so they would have time to walk to church. Then they would walk an hour or two back to their homes. Many were so hungry for God, the opportunity to go to church made the long trip worth it for them.

Even those who lived close to the mission station did not have any way to read the Bible for themselves throughout the week. Imagine the thrill of learning to read and reading the Bible in your own language for the first time. They were so happy when my mom taught them to read so they could begin to read the Bible for themselves. The only reason they even had the scriptures in their language is because my father, with a team, translated the Bible into their language.

My mom also wrote letters to family and friends back home to the U.S.A. She told them stories about the people so they could pray for them. She asked people to send boxes of used clothes for the mission so the African children could have at least one outfit.

My sister, two years younger, and I stood with her and the African children. We sorted through the boxes

of clothes to find the right sizes, or at least something close. The children would wear the clothing item until it wore out. She taught the women basic hygiene, like washing their hands after going to the bathroom to cut down on diseases. She handed out itch medicine to ease their incessant itching from bug bites. She even helped deliver a baby. Through observing her, at a very young age, she taught me to care for others.

Wherever she lived in Africa and later in the U.S.A, she reached out to people in practical ways to show love, compassion, and care. When she owned a preschool after she came to the U.S.A., it was more than a business for her. After hours, she continually counseled and helped the mothers.

She went to a local publishing house and got their Bibles that weren't good enough to sell. She wanted to give the mothers the reassuring message of God's love in the Bibles, she gave them.

All was not ideal. My mother suffered damage from severe childhood abuse from her paternal grandmother. She had many issues to deal with, such as depression and emotional trauma from the severe abuse. I inherited some of those challenges and issues to work through as well. Children often suffer from secondary abuse when their parents haven't healed from theirs.

However, she didn't let her brokenness or any of her emotional challenges stand in her way of caring for others. She modeled an important truth for me as her daughter. You don't have to be perfect or have a perfect life to have a heart to share and care for others. You can still make a significant and positive difference in their lives.

At the end of her life during an especially emotionally challenging time, she told me. "When I'm no longer here, I hope you'll remember the good." This tribute and her letters are a testimony to the vast amount of good she did despite her health challenges.

I hope sharing this will reassure the reader that you don't have to be perfect to do the will of God. Many of the Bible characters had issues as well. All He wants is your "yes" in your heart.

We had family devotions in the evening. My mother tended to go on and on in prayer, pouring out her heart to God. One time my little sister, having grown impatient with the long prayer, said, "In Jesus name, Amen." Then it became a family joke when my mom went on too long for our young minds.

However, she continued to pray. I saw her in her bedroom on her knees beseeching God for herself, family, others, and the work they were doing. One time, when I went astray, I had the realization that my parents' prayers brought me back to faith.

She had an amazing impact on me in shaping the direction of my life. Her example of sharing and caring for others inspires me to this day. I am forever grateful and have done my best to carry on her legacy of care for others.

She died when she was fifty and I was only thirty, so I never did get the chance to tell her these things. Often, it's not until later in life that you realize all your parents have done for you.

Mom, I hope somehow in heaven you can hear my thanks as I honor you. I love you.

# Tribute to Dad
# He Gave the Best Gift

My father gave me one of the best gifts a father could give to his daughter. He modeled his love for God's Word and others. Years ago, in the early fifties, my father heard the voice of God calling him to be a missionary in Congo. In obedience to God's voice, he took his young wife and two little girls into the jungle of Africa. The people there nicknamed them Mama and Papa Obedience.

The image of my father sitting on a kipoi, the African carrying chair, is still vivid in my memory. This was his means of transportation into the jungles of Africa. He did not have the stamina the Africans did to walk for three days.

As he got ready to leave, the sweat gathered under his helmet and ours as we swatted the never-ending flies. Mom tucked several loaves of fresh-baked banana bread into his belongings because banana bread kept longer than most food items. I caught a whiff of the aroma and looked forward to fresh slices of the tasty treat later on.

My dad endured long trips into the interior of the

Dad on a kipoi going into the jungle.

jungle despite the unrelenting heat, threats of gorillas and poisonous snakes. When he arrived at his destination, the people mobbed him, feeling his face, his hair, his arms. They had never seen a white man before. As they stared at this pale creature, they giggled with childlike delight.

He preached the gospel and recruited young men from the jungles to bring them to the mission station. There, he trained them to return to their villages and establish their own churches to spread the good news about God's love.

What motivated him to take his twenty-six-year-old wife and two young daughters to a mission station in the Belgian Congo? One of his favorite Bible verses inspired him: "For Christ's love compels us, because we are convinced that one died for all, and therefore all died" (2 Corinthians 5:14 NIV).

To this day, people benefit from his decision to obey God and to use his gifts, talents, and abilities to serve others. A Congolese man I have never met wept on the phone when he talked to me. He wept out of gratitude for what my father had done for him and his tribe.

When my dad had arrived in Congo, he spent hours and hours first learning the language. Then he worked with a team to translate the Bible into the native tongue. He completed the project before he left the mission station.

Fifty years later, I talked to a grandson of one of the men of that tribe. I won't go into the miraculous details of how the phone conversation happened, but the grandson thanked me profusely for the work my father did. He wept, and I wept as he shared. "I have the Bible in my language today because of what your father did. How wonderful it is to be able to read the Bible in my own native language. My whole tribe can enjoy reading the Bible because of your father's work."

I remember the hardship, the incredible difficulties, and the life-threatening adversities growing up in

Africa. After Congo got its independence, we had to evacuate twice when our lives were threatened. For several years, we lived with constant threats to our lives. When we evacuated the second time, we ended up losing everything we owned.

Overriding all the challenges, my dad's example of service to God and others lives on in my heart. One of my favorite images of my father is the way he got up early every morning to spend time with God. This verse reminds me of my father's dedication. "O God, You *are* my God; Early, will I seek You;" (Psalm 63:1a NKJV)

Throughout the day, in his spare time, he memorized scripture verses. I remember him walking around the house with Bible verses on cards in his hand. The Navigator's discipleship program taught him to do this. When he drove, he kept those cards with the verses close to review them on long trips.

To this day, I love and memorize the Word of God. I started the habit of scripture memorization. I am always reviewing old favorites and memorizing new Bible verses. I used to use 3 x 5 cards but now I use the Bible Memory app, an awesome app that enables you to record, memorize, and review verses.

I have fond memories of my dad reading Bible story comic books to us in the evening. Stories of the Bible

Dad read Bible stories to us.

characters fascinated me. Some of the women inspired me to emulate them, such as Ruth. She inspired me with her kindness, compassion, and loyalty.

My dad didn't use words much. In my teens, I had a broken relationship with him and in my adult years, we reconciled. By his actions, he showed me what was important in life. I know he loved me, and I loved him.

My dad gave me the best gift, a legacy of a man who purposed to love God and others. He highly esteemed the Word of God and taught me to do the same. He made mistakes, and I have made mistakes, some more serious than others. None of us are perfect, and that's why we need a Savior. I keep coming back to what my father modeled for me. I do my best to love God, care for others, focus on work that will last for eternity, memorize and meditate on the Word of God.

So, Dad, I honor you and thank you for teaching me what is important in life! I look forward to seeing you someday when I arrive in heaven. We'll have all those conversations I longed for in the light of how God redeems everything and works them out for good.

In the meantime, I will write my tribute to you. I honor you by focusing on the things you valued the most. I am deeply grateful for the best gifts you gave me.

My dad's actions taught and inspired me to follow Christ's example more than any words he spoke. The love of Christ compelled my father's sacrifice, and now the love of Christ compels me as his daughter.

"All people are like grass, and all their glory is like the flowers of the field; the grass withers and the flowers fall, but the word of the Lord endures forever." (I Peter 1:24, 25 NIV)

# Epilogue

After my parents had to leave Africa, they went to live in Wheaton, Illinois. Dad wanted to go to college and get his degree. He had a Bible School degree, but he wanted to go on and get a college degree. Of course, since they lost everything, they didn't have money. A few people from churches helped in the beginning, but then that came to an end.

My mother decided to support him so he could go to Wheaton College. She sold encyclopedias for a while but then decided to open a private preschool. She did very well with it and became a competent businesswoman and preschool instructor.

She cared for the children and the mothers. She counseled the women and helped them work through their problems. We lived in Wheaton. Since we went to the same church, we knew Ken and Margaret Taylor, who owned the Tyndale Publishing House. Their daughter, Janet, was a good friend of mine. Ken is the one who created the Living Bible paraphrase. He started the paraphrase because he was concerned about his children's difficulty understanding the Bible. At that time, the Bible was mostly the old English King

James Version. He wanted them to have a more understandable version of the Bible. Now Tyndale House publishes the New Living Translation, which is an actual modern translation of the Bible.

With their permission, my mother went to the publishing house and got seconds in good condition. Then she would give them to the mothers of her preschoolers. She had the gift of compassion and did her best to help people. She also continued to tell people about the good news of God's care for them and Jesus's death for their sins.

Dad mowed yards on the weekends and managed an apartment building. With this income and Mom's income, Dad was able to not only finish his degree but also his masters in anthropology. He graduated with honors, in fact with a 4.0. He received an honorary membership in Eta Beta Rho for excellence in Hebraic Scholarship. He made A's in Hebrew. His thesis for his masters was a study comparing Hebrew culture in the Old Testament with that of African tribes with a view to presenting Christianity to them without trying to Westernize them.

After he finished his masters, he got a job at a local junior college teaching anthropology. Unfortunately, he was only able to teach for two years. He had developed ulcerated colitis from having amoebic dysentery in Africa. He took medication for it, but one of the rare side effects created heart problems. He had a genetic heart weakness, and possibly the medication triggered the heart attack.

He had a heart attack in June at age 45 and recovered. A year later, in the same month, June 1974, at age 46, he died of another heart attack. Later, the medical field developed stints and medicine that would have saved him had it happened today.

After my dad finished his masters, my mom went to college and obtained a degree in sociology and graduated with honors. She died four years after my dad. They both died young, but their adult years were exceptionally fruitful for God's Kingdom.

Today, I admire my parents' courage to go into the jungle, initially, and then back into Congo after the first evacuation for four years. They continued to serve God and the African people during the political turmoil. They had life-threatening situations and adversity. At times, their support didn't come as promised. However, they clung to their faith in God's promises and provision during the chaos. Even when they lost all that they owned and their ministry, they did not lose faith.

I also admire my parents' desire to advance themselves. After they returned to the U.S.A, they developed their skills and knowledge to serve others. They had graduated from Bible School before they went to Congo. When they returned to the U.S.A., they both went to college in their later years. Not only that, but they applied themselves to earn honors. They were wonderful role models for me of the value of diligence and hard work!

One of my dad's favorite verses inspires me to this day, "The love of Christ compels us." (2 Corinthians 5:14 NKJV) Their love, courage, and sacrifices motivate and sustain me in my own adversity and ventures in life. I have faced many challenges, including the adoption of seven teenagers from poverty backgrounds.

Now, in responding to a vision God gave me, it is my passion to not only write and share my parents' stories of faith and overcoming adversity, but also mine. Additionally, I want to encourage others to write and share their stories of faith with their children and grandchildren. When the stories are written and shared, they are preserved for generations to come. Those stories can be the seedbed for miracles in future generations.

The Bible admonishes and encourages us to share the works of the Lord from one generation to the next. At the end of this book, I've included many verses to show the importance of sharing our stories of faith. These verses show the importance to God of recording and sharing our faith stories.

# Would you do a favor for me?

If you are enjoying this book, I'd appreciate it if you'd leave a review for this book on Amazon. Go to Amazon.com and type in the title and subtitle of this book. If you can't find it, type in my full name, Sharon Rose Gibson, and all my books will come up. Look for the button that says, "Create your own review" on the right side of the page and click the button to get started.

Positive reviews help more people find the book and spread the message of the important work missionaries do. Hopefully, this book will inspire more to do the good works God calls them to do. If you think of someone who would benefit from this book, tell them about it or buy it as a gift.

Also, if you would like support in writing or editing your own stories, visit www.writeyourstorynow.com or you can email me at info(a) 15minutewriter.com. Additionally, I have a course to teach you to write your stories and several books to encourage you in your writing.

# How to Know God and Go to Heaven

You are valuable and precious to God! He created you with a longing for Him. You have a God-shaped hole in your life that nothing else can fill. He created you in His image to have all the good qualities He has.

The problem is this. Everyone has fallen short of that ideal or sinned in some way. Some people have a problem admitting that they have sinned. But the word sin simply means to fall short. Think about the Ten Commandments. Some people may think these are too legalistic, but God gave them to us to protect us and to help us choose to live in a way that is best for us and others. Here they are in case you are not familiar with them from the book of Exodus, chapter 20 and also Deuteronomy 5 (NKJV).

1. I am the LORD your God; you shall not have strange gods before me.
2. You shall not take the name of the LORD your God in vain.
3. Remember to keep holy the LORD's Day.
4. Honor your father and mother.

5. You shall not kill.
6. You shall not commit adultery.
7. You shall not steal.
8. You shall not bear false witness against your neighbor.
9. You shall not covet your neighbor's wife.
10. You shall not covet your neighbor's goods.

Have you ever told a lie or fudged the truth a little? Have you ever taken something that wasn't yours? Have you ever committed adultery? Maybe you haven't done the physical act, but Jesus said if you even look at someone with lust in your heart, then you have committed adultery. Have you ever cursed using God's name? Have you ever been mean about your neighbor to someone? Have you ever said something unkind that later you regretted?

If you look at these things, everyone can recognize that you have fallen short of the ideal, even if you strive to be good. If you admit that you've sinned, then you are in a great place because you recognize it. Now some people will say, "I can sin and just ask for forgiveness." Let's see how that works. If you owed someone a lot of money or you owed the state large amounts of money in fines, could you go and ask the judge for forgiveness?

Could you say, "Hey, judge, I know I owe all that, but would you forgive me?"

He may say, "Yes, I'll forgive you, but you still have to pay the fine and pay the person that you wronged." This is the same for the judgment day. When you stand before God, you will be judged for what you did. If you continue in your sin and rebellion against God, you will be condemned to an eternal separation from God in a continual state of misery.

However, God saw that this was going to happen. So, He gave His precious only begotten Son, Jesus, to die for our sins. Jesus paid the penalty for every sin you have ever committed or are going to commit. God is a God of justice, but He is also a God of mercy, forgiveness, and second chances. Jesus put Himself through hell so you could be with Him in heaven.

Paul, the apostle, tells us in Hebrews 12:2 (NKJV) that "For the joy set before Him, He endured the cross." Endure is an understatement for the severe beatings and crucifixion Jesus went through for you. For the joy of being able to have you back close to Him here on earth and in heaven instead of going to hell, He went through all He did.

Do you feel some distance between yourself and God? This is because of sin. Sin separates you from God. The Bible tells us that everyone has a conscience. Some people repress it and continue to do bad things which can sear their conscience, but it is still there, along with the sense that there is Someone greater.

As I said earlier, in the heart of every human being is a God-shaped hole with a longing to know their Creator. This is true of you as well. You may be asking, how do I get closer to God?

If your heart is sincere, it's simple but profound. Admit that you are a sinner, that you need a Savior. Ask Him to forgive you and acknowledge that Jesus is Lord. Pray to Him with sincerity in your heart.

He will give you the gift of eternal life. "If you declare with your mouth, Jesus is Lord and believe in your heart that God raised Him from the dead, you will be saved. For it is with your heart that you believe and are justified. and it is with your mouth you profess and are saved." (Romans 10:9, 10 NIV)

Here is a visual to help you see what I've been explaining from the verse, Romans 6:23. This is from The Navigators.

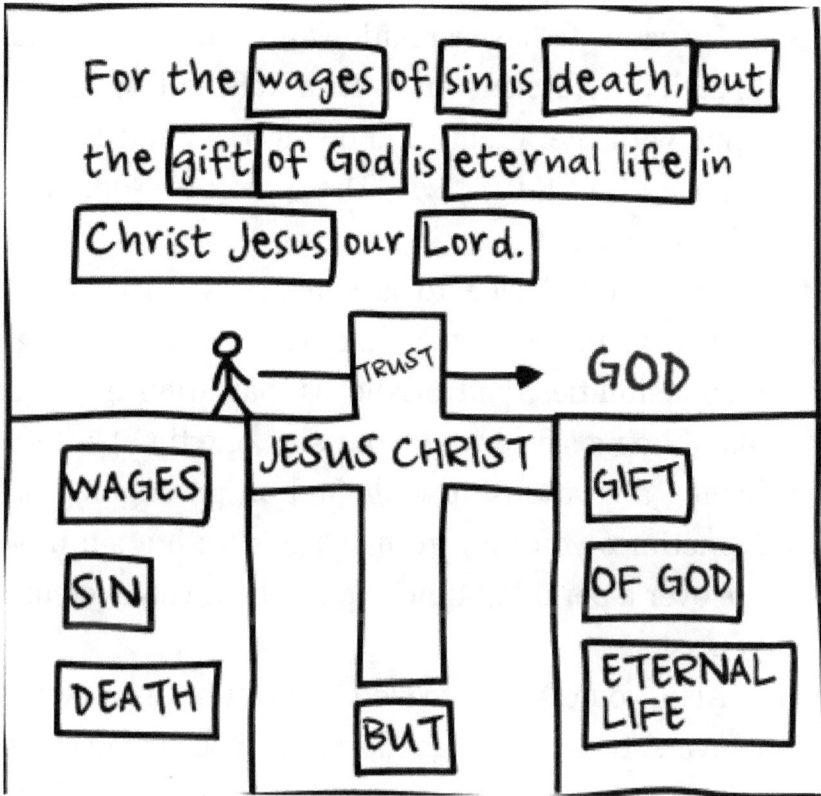

For the wages of sin is death, but the gift of God is eternal life in Christ Jesus our Lord.

TRUST — GOD

JESUS CHRIST

WAGES
SIN
DEATH

GIFT
OF GOD
ETERNAL LIFE

BUT

https://www.navigators.org/resource/one-verse-evangelism

If you come to Him, you must believe that He exists and that He will reward you for seeking Him.

Hebrews 11:6 (NKJV) tells us, "But without faith it is impossible to please Him, for he who comes to God must believe that He is, and that He is a rewarder of those who diligently seek Him."

He wants to have a relationship with you even more than you do. Reach out to Him, talk to Him, read the Bible with the intent of knowing Him and His ways. James 4:8 (NKJV) says, "Draw near to God, and He will draw near to you."

Once you decide to accept Jesus Christ as your Savior, you become a child of God with all the rights, responsibilities, and privileges. Salvation is not only about being saved from your sins one time, but about having a relationship with God on an ongoing basis. Sometimes you may even struggle with a sin in your life over a period of time. He will help you overcome if you ask.

Also, you can talk to God like you have an everyday conversation with a good friend. You have access to ongoing help, provision, and protection in God's Kingdom.

In the next section, I'll share a little about myself as the author and after that I list some key verses relating to writing your stories

# About the Author

You might be curious about how I started on this writing journey. Here's how my love affair with writing started.

I stumbled across a book on how to write in a co-worker's library. The contents lit a candle of passion in me for this wonderful craft. The flame grew brighter and brighter the more I practiced good writing skills.

At the present time, I've been writing for over twenty-five years. I have been published in many anthologies including the Chicken Soup series as well as self-publishing. I delight in refining my writing skills as I've diligently implemented what I've learned.

I have written several books and one book especially to make writing skills simple for those who wanted to write their stories in a captivating way. "Write Your Story NOW: Writing Skills to Captivate Your Reader." You can find all my books at 15minutewriter.com/books.

Later in life, I realized that it was important to share some of my stories about growing up in Africa. Also, as

I mentioned earlier, preserving my mother's and father's legacy is crucial to me. Doing so has been a fascinating and rewarding journey. Not only have I preserved these stories for generations to come, but I have benefited from the process.

I believe you will also find learning how to write your stories to be one of life's most rewarding journeys. I am willing to support you in doing so if you contact me. Send me an email to info(at)15minutewriter.com.

Besides writing, one of my life's missions has been to raise up children from poverty to fulfill their God given potential. My husband, Stan, and I adopted seven teens from poverty backgrounds. This is one of the most challenging and fulfilling things I have done in my life. I like to write stories about those experiences to raise the level of awareness of the value of moving children from poverty to purpose. All of our children have overcome many challenges, and several have children of their own.

I also taught at a ranch for men from poverty backgrounds. God has given me a heart, especially for those in poverty. My parents modeled this for me. Their care for others inspired and motivated me.

Additionally, in my senior years, I am a substitute teacher in my school district. I encourage the students in their studies with support and caring discipline.

As a writer, creative expression is critical, so I explore other creative activities. I encourage you to do the same. Art enraptures my heart. I enjoy painting with watercolor, especially flowers. I do calligraphy and creative lettering and love to experiment with photography.

To keep my mind sharp, I exercise regularly. I take pleasure in eating healthy foods and seeking natural remedies.

Reading improves your writing. I love to read in order to learn and grow as a writer and as a person.

In closing, I'd like to bring to your attention the desperate need for medical care in the Democratic Republic of Congo.

If you would like to support the ongoing work in the Congo, go to https://congonursescholarship.org. Click on donate and then specify that you want the contribution to go to the Congo Nurse Scholarship fund. The funds will be deeply appreciated.

In the next section, I will share with you the many verses in the Bible that encourage us to tell and write our stories and pass them on from one generation to the next.

# God Wants Us to Write and Share Our Stories

This section lists many verses which encourage us to share our stories of faith and what God has done for us. These are a lot of verses showing the heart of God and His desire and admonition to us to write and share our stories.

Think for a moment. Where would we be if the Biblical writers had not bothered to write and share the stories? We wouldn't be inspired, encouraged and taught by them. They greatly enriched us by taking the time to write their God inspired stories.

Even though there are a lot of verses, I urge you to read through them to understand God's desires for you and me. Since there are so many verses, this tells us this is important to God and if it's important to God, it needs to be important to us.

Publish his glorious deeds among the nations. Tell everyone about the amazing things he does. (I Chronicles 16:24 NLT)

I will give thanks to you, LORD, with all my heart; I will tell of all your wonderful deeds. I will be glad and rejoice in you; I will sing the praises of your name, O Most High. (Psalm 9:1,2 NIV)

Let the redeemed of the Lord tell their story—those he redeemed from the hand of the foe. (Psalm 17:2 NIV)

For what you have done I will always praise you in the presence of your faithful people. And I will hope in your name, for your name is good. (Psalm 52:9 NIV)

Come and hear, all you who fear God; let me tell you what he has done for me. (Psalm 66:16 NIV)

The Lord announces the word, and the women who proclaim it are a mighty throng: (Psalm 68:11 NIV)

My mouth will tell of your righteous deeds, of your saving acts all day long though I know not how to relate all of them.

I will come and proclaim your mighty acts, Sovereign Lord; I will proclaim your righteous deeds, yours alone.

Since my youth, Lord, you have taught me and to this day, I declare your marvelous deeds. Even when I'm old and gray, do not forsake me, my God, till I declare your power to the next generation, your mighty acts to all who are to come. (Psalm 71:15-18 NIV)

But as for me, it is good to be near God. I have made the Sovereign Lord my refuge; I will tell of all your deeds. (Psalm 73:28 NIV)

We praise you Lord for your name is near; people tell of your wonderful deeds. (Psalm75:1 NIV)

I will remember the works of the LORD, yes, I will remember Your wonders of old. I will reflect on all You have done and ponder Your mighty deeds. (Psalm 77: 10, 11 NIV)

My people, hear my teaching; listen to the words of my mouth. I will open my mouth with a parable; I will utter hidden things, things from of old– things we have heard and known, things our ancestors have told us.

We will not hide them from their descendants; we will tell the next generation the praiseworthy deeds of the Lord, his power, and the wonders he has done.

He decreed statutes for Jacob and established the law in Israel, which he commanded our ancestors to teach their children, so the next generation would know them, even the children yet to be born, and they in turn would tell their children.

Then they would put their trust in God and would not forget his deeds but would keep his commands. (Psalm 78:1-7 NIV)

For you make me glad by your deeds, Lord. I sing for joy at what your hands have done. How great are your works, Lord, how profound are your thoughts! (Psalm 92:4,5 NIV)

Oh, sing to the Lord a new song. Sing to the Lord all the earth. Sing to the Lord, bless His name; Proclaim the good news of His salvation from day to day.
Declare His glory among the nations, His wonders among all peoples. (Psalm 96:1-3 NIV)

Let this be written for a future generation, that a people not yet created may praise the Lord: (Psalm 102:18 NIV)

Give praise to the Lord, proclaim his name; make known among the nations what he has done. (Psalm 105:1 NIV)

Great is the Lord and most worthy of praise; his greatness no one can fathom.

One generation commends your works to another; they tell of your mighty acts.

They speak of the glorious splendor of your majesty—and I will meditate on your wonderful works.

They tell of the power of your awesome works—and I will proclaim your great deeds.

They celebrate your abundant goodness and joyfully sing of your righteousness. (Psalm 145:3-7 NIV)

Go now, write it on tablet for them, inscribe it on a scroll, that for the days to come it may be an everlasting witness. (Isaiah 30:8 NIV)

This is what the Lord, the God of Israel, says: 'Write in a book all the words I have spoken to you." (Jeremiah 30:2 NIV)

Then the Lord answered me and said: "Write the vision and make *it* plain on tablets, that he may run who reads it." (Habakkuk 2:2 NKJV)

For everything that was written in the past was written to teach us, so that through the endurance taught in the scriptures and the encouragement they provide we might have hope. (Romans 15:4 KJV)

So, I will always remind you of these things, even though you know them and are firmly established in the truth you now have. I think it is right to refresh your memory as long as I live in the tent of this body, (I Peter 1:12,13 NIV)

And I will make every effort to see that after my departure you will always be able to remember these things. (I Peter 1:15 NIV)

They triumphed over him by the blood of the Lamb and the word of their testimony; they did not love their lives so much as to shrink from death. (Revelation 12:11 NIV)

He who was seated on the throne said, "I am making everything new!" Then he said, "Write this down, for these words are trustworthy and true." (Revelation 21:5 NIV)

www.ingramcontent.com/pod-product-compliance
Lightning Source LLC
LaVergne TN
LVHW052021080426
835513LV00018B/2102